GOD'S DESIGN FOR "THE CHURCH"

Book 1 in this series:

What Is "the Church"?

GOD'S DESIGN FOR
"THE CHURCH"

Clarifying the Nature
& Intention of
the New Testament Church

Eddie Cloer

RESOURCE ☐
PUBLICATIONS

202 S. Locust
Searcy, AR 72143

ISBN: 0-945441-19-3

Dedication

To my father-in-law,
Otis E. Finn,
A Christian gentleman,
A devoted father to his children,
A faithful, loving husband to his wife,
A wonderful father-in-law to his
sons-in-law and daughter-in-law,
But, most of all, an humble servant of God.

*"The steps of a man are established by the Lord;
and He delights in his way" (Psalms 37:23).*

Contents

Foreword

The apostle Paul described the spirit of our time when he said, "For if the trumpet give an uncertain sound, who shall prepare himself to the battle?" In this century we have seen great changes taking place among the denominations. At the World Missionary Conference held in Edinburgh in 1910, there were delegates present representing the major Protestant bodies. The slogan that characterized this conference was "The Evangelization of the World in this Generation." While there were some dissenters, the prevailing view of Protestantism held to the essentiality of the proclamation of Christ to the world. He was the only means given by God for the salvation of the lost of the world.

Just eighteen years later in 1928, another world missionary conference was held in Jerusalem. A different spirit pervaded this meeting. Secularism was identified as the great enemy of all religious people. The churches represented there were urged to band together with those of other world religions to withstand this common enemy.

This liberal attitude became even more pronounced four years later when the Laymen's Foreign Missions Enquiry was published in 1932. This rethinking of missions advanced the idea that Protestant missionaries should not go into foreign lands to convert other religious people, but rather to do Christian works. If there were ideas innate to Christianity that proved beneficial to these religious neighbors, then they could be shared. However, church representatives should be equally willing to accept positive contributions that other world religions might offer to them.

Especially in the post-World War II era, churches of Christ have witnessed what appears to be similar attitudinal changes on the part of some believers. This movement began as an effort to return to the church of the New Testament, and to find comfort and security in the Christ of Scripture. However, in some sectors, we are witnessing increasing uncertainty as to the finality of this time-honored message.

In the light of Paul's warning, we would do well to remember that uncertain sounds neither prepare one for battle, nor do they attract other volunteers! The Christ of the New Testament was noted as one who "taught them as having authority, and not as the scribes" (Matthew 7:29).

Dr. Eddie Cloer has heralded a "certain sound" in the pages of this book. In the spirit of Jeremiah, who urged the people of his day to "ask for the old paths, where is the good way, and walk therein" (Jeremiah 6:16), Dr. Cloer has brought our attention back to the nature of the "called-out of Christ." By exploring the many biblical titles for the company of the committed, the kingdom of Christ on earth, he has reaffirmed the excitement and the urgency of the church of the New Testament. Once more he brings us face to face with the exclusiveness of the Christ of God, and the salvation which only He is entitled to offer.

This book is a natural extension of the life-work of this man of God. In my office near his at Harding University, I am aware of Dr. Cloer's tireless ministries in both the spoken and the written word. Generations of people who have gotten a vision of God's love and purpose through the ministry of this servant of Christ will rise up to call him blessed! *God's Design for "the Church"* will be a priceless treasure for those who are interested in returning to the plan of God for the identity and the mission of the church in the world as these are so clearly presented in the Bible.

Not only has Dr. Cloer written a very timely and Scripture-based book, but he has written it in such a way that it will serve the church as a study guide. Questions for discussion have been placed at the end of each chapter. At the end of the book, there is an exhaustive presentation of Scriptures which fully explore the subject matter under discussion. This will prove to be a fine basic text for missionaries, preachers, Bible class teachers, and all those who hold the vision of returning to be just the New Testament church.

Carl G. Mitchell

Preface

"The church," or the kingdom of God on earth, is one of the overarching topics of the Scriptures. Therefore, we should study the subject with only one aim in mind: to ascertain God's divine purpose for "the church" in His plan for the salvation of the world. We cannot hope to achieve this all-important aspiration, however, unless we approach the study with pure hearts that are free from all prejudice, human loyalties, and selfish ambitions. Our resolve must be that we will permit nothing to interfere with God's authority over us. His Word, and that Word alone, must be given the first, middle, and final voice on what His eternal purpose is for "the church."

My intent for this book is for it to address and offer insight into two lamentable conditions. For diverse reasons confusion prevails on the meaning of "the church." Popular definitions of "the church" range from denominations to a physical building to a social club to a body of believers in Christ. With many religious people, no identity crisis is being suffered, for they never set out in the first place to fulfill God's design for "the church." Apparently they have given no real thought to what "the church" was intended to be. They have a kind of relationship with Christ but have never sought to be the biblical entity called "the church." This is tragic.

What is even more tragic is the realization that some who entered "the church" at the beginning of their spiritual journey and have lived for some time as "the church" are presently in the throes of an identity crisis. They once knew who they were, but they have lost that vision for one reason or another. This is a dreadful development indeed, for when Christians are unsure of who they are and who they are supposed to be, God's plan for the church obviously cannot be fulfilled. God's design for "the church" will never be implemented by accident. It must be lived out by those who know, on the basis of Scripture, what God wants His people to be and do and how He wants them to be identified in the world.

Writing is an exacting task, one which requires the kind assistance of many friends before completion. The writing of this book is no exception. I am especially grateful to my wife, Susan, who has ever been my faithful coworker in all of my efforts and without whom none of my dreams would have been brought to life; to Cheryl Schramm, our professional typographer and final proofreader and consultant, who has been a precious inspiration to both Susan and me; to Patty Barrett, a genuine Christian friend, who has given assistance on dozens of details that must be done before a book can be finalized; and to Dr. Carl G. Mitchell, the Dean of the College of Bible and Religion at Harding University, who has been a constant encouragement to me and was willing to write the foreword to this book.

All books of this kind are human productions and

contain the imperfections of human frailty. While writing this book, I sought to remain as free from prejudice as possible; I trust that as you read it, you will try to be as free from prejudice as you are capable of being. Let us both, author and reader, reach for the Lord's ideal as revealed in the Scriptures. Let us not be satisfied with anything less than what the Lord desires and delights in. Accept what is written here only if it expresses the truth of His Word.

Dear heavenly Father,

You have given Your Son to redeem us and to purchase the church. Purify our hearts that we might have only one longing in life—living through Jesus as Your church according to Your holy purpose. Forgive us for being selfish and prejudiced. Give us courage to break loose from anything that shackles us and prevents us from being the people of Your own possession. Smite our complacency in living as the world lives and thinking as it thinks. Clarify our vision, that we might see clearly Your plan and direction. May we honor You, Your precious Son, and the blessed Holy Spirit by being—in designation and life—the church of Christ.

In Christ's name, Amen.

"Blessed be the God and Father of our Lord Jesus Christ, who according to His great mercy has caused us to be born again to a living hope through the resurrection of Jesus Christ from the dead, . . ." (1 Peter 1:3).

Eddie Cloer

Prologue

How Did Christ Establish His Church?

One distinctive quality of the earthly life of Christ is that He chose to own almost nothing. We never read in the New Testament of His building a house, renovating a building of any kind, or buying land. The Gospels never refer to Him as purchasing anything—clothing, tools, or even food. While He was present in this world and was, in a sense, a citizen of it, He was never at home in it. He was in the world, but the world was not in Him; He lived in the world as a part of it, but He never allowed it to live in Him. While He lived here, He was a stranger in a foreign land, a pilgrim whose affections and life were absorbed with another world.

Christ rarely used the possessive pronouns "My" and "Mine." He did speak of "disciples of Mine" (John 8:31), "My Father" (Matthew 26:39), "My body" (Matthew 26:26), "My blood" (Matthew 26:28), "My words," (Luke 6:47), and "My church" (Matthew 16:18). Even His references to His body, blood, and words were in a spiritual context with no purely personal aspiration evident.

According to the Gospels, Christ sought to leave

behind as a permanent extension of His earthly ministry only one personal possession, His church—not a college, a physical house, or a fortune (Matthew 16:18). He began His earthly ministry by preaching the coming of the kingdom of God (Matthew 4:17), and He ended it by preaching about the kingdom (Acts 1:3). He indicated that the church He established would be the earthly form of the kingdom of God; thus, in this sense, He could equate the kingdom of God with His church (Matthew 16:16-18).

Since the church is the only entity that Christ sought to own, the only possession that Christ actually left behind, it follows that the church was of singular importance to Him and should be to us. Our dominating desire should be to become and live as His church.

In light of all this, one question is paramount to each of us: "How can we enter His church and live as His church?" This question will be answered for us if we discover how Christ established His church in the beginning. When we see how Christ actually established His church, we will be convinced that we can establish His church today in those places where it does not exist, and we will realize that we can live as faithful members of it wherever we are.

In keeping with the promise He had made, Christ established His church on Pentecost, following His resurrection (Matthew 16:18; Acts 2). How did He do it?

BY THE PREACHING OF THE GOSPEL

The first step in Jesus' plan to establish His church was the preaching of the gospel. The "glad tidings" or "good news" of salvation through God's grace was made known in a public proclamation to the Jews who had gathered on the Day of Pentecost.

This historic day began with the outpouring of the Holy Spirit upon the apostles. Christ had promised such an outpouring, and now that promise had been fulfilled (Acts 1:4, 5; 2:1-4). As a result, the apostles, empowered by this baptism of the Holy Spirit, spoke the wonderful words of God in all the different dialects of those who were present (Acts 2:6-8, 11). Then, as a partial fulfillment of the promise that Christ had made to him (Matthew 16:19), Peter preached a detailed sermon about the deity of Christ (Acts 2:14-36, 40).

As an introduction to his sermon, Peter showed the multitude that what was happening on that day was the heart of the fulfillment of a prophecy made by Joel (Acts 2:15-21). The body of his sermon focused on how Christ had been proven to be both Lord and Christ through His miracles (Acts 2:22), His resurrection (Acts 2:24), His fulfillment of prophecy (Acts 2:25-31; 34, 35), witnesses (Acts 2:32), and the descent of the Holy Spirit (Acts 2:33). Peter concluded his address with the decisive conclusion, "Therefore let all the house of Israel know for certain that God has made Him both Lord and Christ—this Jesus whom you crucified" (Acts 2:36).

On that Day of Pentecost, the world's eyes were probably focused on the activities of the Roman Empire, but from heaven's view the most momentous event in the world was taking place in Jerusalem: The gospel was being preached for the first time! All of God's planning, all the prophecies of the Old Testament era, all the preparation of the earthly life and ministry of Christ had converged, merged, and emerged into the preaching of the gospel of God's grace. The new covenant had been put into effect, and the gospel in its fullness had become a reality.

The preaching of this message must have been an event that caused the devil and all his ambassadors to tremble and all heaven to rejoice. Christ brought His church into being through this preaching of His gospel; and from this time forward, His church will be established in other places of the world by the preaching of the same message.

Think about the significance of the preaching of the gospel by imagining the following scene. Appearing before God's throne on the Day of Judgment is a man who was completely irreligious in life. He never sought the Lord's will, never worshiped God, and never made an attempt to live the Christian life. He went about his life as if he had no obligation to God at all, working at his job, engaging in entertainment, rearing a family, and keeping up with the community in which he lived. As he stands before the throne of judgment, God says, "One time during your life you really made a difference in My work on earth." The man is totally surprised. He replies, "Lord, You know I was not religious at all. I went to a few religious services over the span of my life, but I did not really worship in any of them. My life was a selfish one, devoted entirely to my own plans and purposes. I am not conscious of ever having worked for You on earth. When did I make such a difference in Your work?"

God tells the man, "You owned a little one-stop store on the corner of a main intersection in the town where you lived. One day a man stopped at that store and asked you, 'Can you tell me where the church of Christ meets in this town? I'm sure they meet near here.' You gave him directions to the church's meeting place. That man was one of My preachers. He arrived at the assembly that morning in time to preach My gospel of grace, through which I did My saving work in those who listened and responded to it. You did not know it at the time, but you were a small connecting link in the highest work that was going on in the world. The world thought that what was happening in Washington, D.C., or some other national capital was the most important event occurring in the world, but the most far-reaching event was happening in the little church building when My gospel of salvation was being preached. Your giving directions enabled one of My preachers to preach the gospel to a group of people. That was the greatest thing you ever did."

Paul wrote, "For since in the wisdom of God the world through its wisdom did not come to know God, God was well-pleased through the foolishness of the message preached to save those who believe" (1 Corinthians 1:21). Peter's preaching in Acts 2 brought into effect the last will and testament of Christ and inaugurated the Christian Age. Dr. James D. Bales has called Acts 2 "The Hub of the Bible"; all that goes before Acts 2 looks forward to it, and all that follows Acts 2 looks backward to it. Without question, he is correct.

The beginning of the church revolved around the preaching of the gospel. The church of Christ which was established on this Day of Pentecost can be established where it does not exist only by the preaching of the same gospel that Peter preached. To express it another way, one farmer can grow the same variety of tomatoes as another farmer only if he plants the same type of tomato seed that the other farmer planted. To have the same church that Christ built, we must preach the same gospel by which Christ built it in the beginning.

BY THE OBEYING OF THE GOSPEL

The second step in Jesus' plan to establish His church was the obeying of the gospel. His church would never have been established if the people present had not obeyed the gospel which was preached.

Peter drew the evidence of his sermon to a specific conclusion which all honest hearts must accept: that Jesus had been made "both Lord and Christ" (Acts 2:36). Then a crowd of listeners cried, "What shall we do?" (Acts 2:37). Their hearts were "pierced," or broken, by the Word of God; they were convicted by the Holy Spirit through the preached Word. Peter did not create their guilt through his method of preaching; he exposed it through the revealing Word which pierces as far as the division of soul and spirit, of both joints and marrow, and judges the thoughts and intentions of the heart (Hebrews 4:12).

To those Jews who cried out with smitten consciences and broken hearts, Peter gave this answer: "Repent, and let each of you be baptized in the name of Jesus Christ for the forgiveness of your sins; and you shall receive the gift of the Holy Spirit" (Acts 2:38). Christ had named three conditions of salvation in His last commission to His apostles: faith, repentance, and baptism (Mark 16:15, 16; Luke 24:46, 47; Matthew 28:19, 20). Peter did not mention faith in his answer to their question, because their cry for directions indicated that faith had been engendered by the sermon they had heard. He specified two conditions that they still needed to meet: repentance and baptism. The forgiveness they craved and cried out for would be granted through Christ's blood upon their compliance with those commands. Then, as saved people, they would be given heaven's gift, the Holy Spirit.

Luke recorded, "So then, those who had received his word were baptized; and there were added that day about three thousand souls" (Acts 2:41). The apostles were set in the church as part of its foundation (Ephesians 2:20). As these three thousand completed their obedience to the gospel, they were spiritually cemented together and placed by the Holy Spirit on the foundation of Jesus Christ and the apostles (1 Corinthians 3:11). Thus, the church was born, or brought into existence. From that day to this, anytime anyone obeys the same gospel that the three thousand obeyed, he is added to the same church, and the superstructure of the church which rests upon the foundation of Jesus and the apostles grows higher.

In May 1993, twenty-five Christians participated in a campaign for Christ in Donetsk, Ukraine. Our intent was to establish the Lord's church in that city. We blended together personal teaching, television preaching, and nightly preaching in a lecture hall. In our preaching and teaching we sought to teach the same gospel that Peter preached on the Day of Pentecost. We asked people to become Christians the same way Peter did—by faith, repentance, and baptism. During the ten-day campaign, 122 people expressed their desire to become Christians. Thirty-five people came on one night. We stressed to all those who came to be baptized that they were not entering a denomination; rather, through their sincere obedience to the gospel of Christ, they were being added by the Lord to His church, the church He established on Pentecost.

This new church of Christ rented the second floor of a theater as a meeting place. On the last Lord's Day we were with them, the rented room was filled to capacity and beyond. We rejoiced in our salvation through

Christ's death as we observed the Lord's Supper together, sang together, prayed together, gave out of our prosperity, and listened to the preaching of the gospel.

In ten short days, the church was established in Donetsk by bringing honest-hearted people into the kingdom of God through the preaching of the gospel and the obeying of the gospel. These 122 people were added to the church which our dear Lord established on the Day of Pentecost as recorded in Acts 2.

Suppose we had conducted this campaign, with its preaching, teaching, and meetings, but no one had obeyed the gospel. Would the church have been established in Donetsk? The answer is obvious, is it not? It would not have been established. Regardless of good intentions, elaborate plans, and personal dedication, the church cannot exist unless people obey the gospel of the New Testament.

Christ established His church when three thousand obeyed His gospel. His church can be established in any place where it does not exist today through the preaching of the gospel that Peter preached and through people's obedience to that same gospel. Christ established His church in this way in the beginning, and this is the only way it can be established today.

BY THE LIVING OF THE GOSPEL

The third step in Jesus' plan to establish His church could be called the living of the gospel. The people who obeyed the gospel lived it daily; thus, Christ's church throbbed with life.

Luke said of those who had become Christians, "And they were continually devoting themselves to the apostles' teaching and to fellowship, to the breaking of bread and to prayer" (Acts 2:42). Not only did they become Christ's church, but they lived from that day on as Christ's church.

The lives of these early Christians illustrate that living the gospel requires commitment. They devoted themselves to the apostles' teaching, to fellowship, to the breaking of bread, and to prayer. They did not begin and then quickly fizzle out; they started and remained steadfastly committed to the truth of God. They worshiped God regularly; worship became a way of life for them. Becoming a Christian was like turning onto a new road on which they would walk the rest of their lives.

Living the gospel demanded compassion. Luke said, "And they began selling their property and possessions, and were sharing them with all, as anyone might have need" (Acts 2:45). They did not ask of others, "Will you help me?" Rather, they asked those among them who were in need, "May I help you?" The compassionate Christ lived in them, and that compassion was expressed in their motives and deeds.

The first Christians also lived the gospel by keeping its unity. Luke wrote, "And all those who had believed were together, and had all things in common" (Acts 2:44). He later added, "And the congregation of those who believed were of one heart and soul; . . ." (Acts 4:32). They had been knitted together into spiritual oneness by the Spirit of God when they obeyed the gospel, and they were maintaining that unity by loyalty to the Spirit's message, unfeigned unselfishness, and genuine concern for one another.

The church of Christ can exist anywhere people are willing to listen to the gospel, obey it, and live it. When I attended Harding College years ago, I sometimes drove to Springfield, Arkansas, and preached. The church there was small, but what it lacked in size, it made up for in spirit. This church was made up of about twelve women. Having no men in the congregation, the women had to carry on the work by themselves. My roommate, Terry Seaman, would go with me, and we would lead the entire service. When I preached, Terry would lead the singing, word the prayers, and serve the Lord's Supper. When Terry preached, I would take care of the rest of the service.

These women were in a difficult circumstance. They had no one to help them, but they continued steadfastly as Christ's church. When they did not have a preacher, as on Wednesday nights, they would sing, pray, and study the Bible as a group of Christian women. They continued to live the gospel, even though their circumstances were not ideal.

If you should ever visit Springfield, Arkansas, you will find that the church of Christ is still meeting and serving. You will find the church to be strong and active. It is still not very big, but it is faithful and steadfast. The church in Springfield would probably not exist if it were not for those faithful women who daily lived the gospel, even in their difficult situation. They knew what it took for the church to live in a community.

We have often heard of campaigns during which several people were baptized. They were born into the kingdom of God by the Spirit of God, and the church of Christ began meeting. It looked as though the church had been established in that place. When the campaign ended and the campaigners went home, however, the new Christians became discouraged. Soon the attendance at their worship services dwindled, and finally the church ceased to meet. Everyone quit living the gospel, and the church passed out of existence in that place. The church of Christ simply cannot survive where the gospel is not lived.

Christ established His church on Pentecost through people who would live the gospel, and His church is established where it does not exist today in the same way. There are no exceptions to this rule. If the church is to live in our community, we must obey the gospel and live it.

CONCLUSION

How, then, did Christ establish His church? He did it through the gospel's being preached, obeyed, and lived. The application for us is obvious: The church is established the same way today. Where the same gospel is preached, the same gospel is obeyed, and the same gospel is lived, the same church that Christ established on Pentecost is established and lives.

Obey the gospel of the New Testament, live it daily, and you will be the church of Christ.

The story is told of a preacher who was delivering a sermon on marriage. He was hammering this thought: "You know God's plan: just one man for one woman, and just one woman for one man. That is His plan. You cannot improve on it." For almost an hour he went over and over his point. When the service ended and he was greeting each worshiper at the door, he met two spinsters. It was obvious that the opportunities for marriage were about to pass these women by. They said, "Preacher, we don't want to improve on it. We just want to get in on it!"

Are these not your sentiments regarding Christ's church? You cannot improve on it. He knows you better than you know yourself. He designed His church for your needs. Any change made in Christ's church removes its divine perfection and replaces it with human frailty.

Take Christ as He is and, by obeying and living His gospel, become the very church He built.

For Preaching and Teaching Purposes: Sermon or Teaching Type: Basic pattern; deductive; expository. Subject: The church. Theme: How Christ established His church. Title: How Did Christ Establish His Church? Preaching or Teaching Portion: Acts 2. Proposition: (Declarative/didactic) We can be the church of Christ today. Interrogative Question or Probing Question: How? Key Word: Steps. Major Points: I. By the Preaching of the Gospel; II. By the Obeying of the Gospel; III. By the Living of the Gospel. Sermonic or Teaching Objective: To persuade people to be the church of Christ.

1

The Kingdom of God

"For He delivered us from the domain of darkness, and transferred us to the kingdom of His beloved Son" (Colossians 1:13).

Someone has said, "The ocean is deep enough for an elephant to swim in but shallow enough for a child to wade on its shores." Indeed, the ocean does have many different characteristics. It has shoreline and shallow waters, yet it has mammoth depths and a sprawling, incredible width.

Likewise, the church of the New Testament has numerous features. When we contemplate its unity of function and our union with Christ, we see the church as the body of Christ (Romans 12:5). When we think of the warmth, support, and companionship which we receive as His church, we view it as the family of God (Ephesians 2:19). When we think of it from the viewpoint of the rule and reign of God, we recognize it as the kingdom of God on earth (Matthew 16:16-18).

These different descriptions do not conflict with

each other, but rather blend together to illustrate the composite nature of the divine organism which we call (by translation) the church. The glory of the New Testament church is that inherent within it are a multitude of holy traits which Christ provided through the cross.

Unquestionably, the Holy Spirit wants us to view the church as a kingdom. Paul spoke of conversion to Christ as a translation from the kingdom of darkness into the kingdom of Christ: "For He delivered us from the domain of darkness, and transferred us to the kingdom of His beloved Son" (Colossians 1:13). Since conversion is described elsewhere in the New Testament as entrance into the body of Christ (e.g., Romans 6:3; Galatians 3:27) and since the body of Christ is spoken of as the church (Ephesians 1:21-23), it follows that the Holy Spirit intends for us to see the church, the body of Christ, and the kingdom of Christ (or the kingdom of God) as the same spiritual organism.

The word "kingdom" is used in at least six contexts in the Bible. (1) It is used in reference to an earthly, secular, governmental rule (Matthew 4:8). (2) It is used to convey the concept of "the reign of God" in the Old and New Testaments. When God formally made Israel into His chosen nation, He identified it as His kingdom (Exodus 19:5, 6). (3) It is used regarding the rule or power of God (Matthew 12:28). Wherever the will of God is obeyed, the reign of God or the kingdom of God exists. (4) It is used of God's reign in heaven. As Peter urged us to grow in the Christian virtues, he referred to heaven as the eternal kingdom of our Lord: "For in this way the entrance into the eternal kingdom of our Lord and Savior Jesus Christ will be abundantly supplied to you" (2 Peter 1:11). (5) It is applied to the church. The church is God's earthly manifestation of His heavenly kingdom. Therefore, it is referred to as the kingdom of heaven (Matthew 16:18, 19), the kingdom of God (John 3:5), and the kingdom of His beloved Son (Colossians 1:13). (6) The word is used in reference to the dominion of Satan. His power is conveyed by the phrase "Satan's kingdom" (Matthew 12:26).[1]

It is both encouraging and intriguing to reflect upon the church as the kingdom of God. In particular, let us focus on the characteristics of the Lord's earthly kingdom, the church.

A SPIRITUAL KINGDOM

In its basic nature, the church is a spiritual kingdom, not a physical or material one. When Pilate asked Jesus, "Are You the King of the Jews?" (John 18:33), Jesus responded by saying, "My kingdom is not of this world. If My kingdom were of this world, then My servants would be fighting, that I might not be delivered up to the Jews; but as it is, My kingdom is not of this realm" (John 18:36).

This spiritual nature of the kingdom introduces vital truths regarding the church. First, the headquarters of the church are in heaven, not on earth. Christ, our sovereign King, sits at God's right hand in heaven (Acts 2:33). He will reign as King of God's earthly kingdom, the church, until the end of time,

---

[1]Appendix 2 in the book *What Is "the Church"?* includes all the references in the New Testament to the words "kingdom" and "kingdoms." These references should be helpful in understanding how the New Testament uses these words. The word "kingdom" is used 152 times in the New Testament, and the word "kingdoms" is used 3 times. See Eddie Cloer, *What Is "the Church"?* (Searcy, Ark.: Resource Publications, 1993), 187-213.

when He will deliver the kingdom up to God, the Father (1 Corinthians 15:24). Thus, Christians are people who have entered the rule of God by submitting to the Lordship of Jesus (Philippians 2:9-11).

Second, Christians' lives, work, and worship center on the spiritual, not the physical. We wage a spiritual warfare (Ephesians 6:12), offer up spiritual sacrifices to God (1 Peter 2:5), live on spiritual food (Hebrews 5:12-14), and live in this world as pilgrims whose citizenship is in heaven (Philippians 3:20; 1 Peter 2:11).

We are true citizens of the kingdom of God when God rules and reigns over our hearts.

Third, as members of this spiritual kingdom, our relationships with the material realities of this world are governed by our spiritual citizenship in the kingdom of heaven. We see the worthlessness of the tinsel of this life when we view it through the lens of eternity.

Someone has proposed an imaginary conversation between a Christian and the devil. The devil says, "I'll give you everything, Mr. Christian. I'll give you houses, lands, and money." Mr. Christian responds by saying, "I have everything. My Father owns the world and all that's in it. You can't give me anything, because I have everything." The devil tries again: "I'll take everything away from you. I'll take your house, your pleasures, and your money." Mr. Christian responds, "You can't take anything away from me. I don't have anything. All I have has been given to God. I belong to His spiritual kingdom, so my true values are spiritual in nature." The devil tries still another time: "I'll kill you.

I'll take away your life." Mr. Christian says, "For to me to live is Christ and to die is gain." The devil makes one final try: "I'll make you live in misery. You will look at all the pleasurable things which sinners are doing, and you will be unable to do them. You will live in discontent." Mr. Christian declares, "My highest joy is doing the will of Jesus." Being a member of God's spiritual kingdom puts this world and its temptations in a different light. It helps us to say with John, "And the world is passing away, and also its lusts; but the one who does the will of God abides forever" (1 John 2:17).

Citizens of the kingdom of heaven do not view this world as do the people of the world. Those who belong only to this world must worry about their possessions, their present and future, and world affairs. Christians are *in the world*, but we *do not belong to it*. We belong to a spiritual kingdom, not this physical one. Our devotion is spiritual, not secular. While we minister to the sick, feed the hungry, and work to make the world a better place to live, our hearts' real concerns are eternal. We pursue above all other interests the spiritual salvation of each person we meet. We live for spiritual goals, not worldly ones. Men of this world sell new suits; Christians seek new souls.

A KINGDOM OF RIGHTEOUSNESS

Second, the church is a kingdom of righteousness. Citizens of the kingdom of heaven do not live as they lived formerly, before entering this kingdom. Paul said that the children of the kingdom are the children of light: "For you were formerly darkness, but now you are light in the Lord; walk as children of light (for the fruit of the light consists in all goodness and righteousness and truth), trying to learn what is pleasing to the Lord" (Ephesians 5:8-10). He further said, "For the kingdom of God is not eating and drinking, but righteousness and peace and joy in the Holy Spirit" (Romans 14:17).

The New Testament speaks of two kinds of righteousness. One is *an extended righteousness,* which is often spoken of by the inspired writers. When we become Christians, this righteousness is bestowed upon us and we are justified before God. In conversion to Christ, we are "justified as a gift by His grace through the redemption which is in Christ Jesus" (Romans 3:24).

The New Testament also refers to *an exhibited righteousness.* Christians are to walk in, or habitually manifest, righteousness. John wrote, ". . . the one who practices righteousness is righteous, just as He is righteous" (1 John 3:7). It is so unthinkable for Christians to "live in" or "walk in" sin that John said, "The one who practices sin is of the devil; . . . No one who is born of God practices sin, . . ." (1 John 3:8, 9). The kingdom of God, therefore, is a kingdom of righteousness; righteousness is extended to those who enter it, and righteousness is exhibited by those who live as true citizens of it.

The rule and reign of God in the heart manifests itself in righteousness in the life. The story is told of a man who lived during the Great Depression of the 1930s in the USA. He was a member of the church who was not affected to any degree by the depression. While others suffered in poverty, he lived in comfort and wealth. On Sunday mornings, however, when the collection plate passed him, he put in a dime. In that day, the church was in desperate need of his financial assistance to do the work of Christ in the world, but he consistently gave only a dime. Apparently, he was in the kingdom but the kingdom was not in him.

We are true citizens of the kingdom of God when God rules and reigns over our hearts. The kingdom of God is a kingdom of righteousness. Citizenship in this kingdom means a recognition of the sovereignty of God and a submission to His will in our daily lives.

AN ETERNAL KINGDOM

Third, the church is God's eternal kingdom on earth. It is not fleeting or temporary; it is stable, unshakable, and everlasting.

Daniel prophesied that the God of heaven would set up a kingdom which would never be destroyed (Daniel 2:44). When Gabriel revealed to Mary that she would be the earthly mother of the Messiah, he mentioned the eternal quality of the kingdom over which the Messiah would reign: "He will be great, and will be called the Son of the Most High; and the Lord God will give Him the throne of His father David; and He will reign over the house of Jacob forever; and His kingdom will have no end" (Luke 1:32, 33). When Jesus announced His intention to establish His church, He promised that the gates of Hades would not overpower it (Matthew 16:18). The kingdom of God is described in Hebrews 12:28 as a kingdom which cannot be shaken.

As citizens of the kingdom of heaven, Christians possess eternal life. This life is both *an experience now* and *an expectation for the future*. All who possess Jesus have eternal life now, for He is the very embodiment of eternal life (1 John 1:2). Consequently, John wrote, "Everyone who hates his brother is a murderer; and you know that no murderer has eternal life *abiding* in him" (1 John 3:15; emphasis mine). The eternal nature of the kingdom of God expresses itself in the quality of life which we experience now as Christians and in the eternal life which we expect to receive in eternity.

Our entrance into eternal life has been likened to a baby's entrance into the world from his mother's womb. The baby experiences life in the environment of the womb. His experience of life, however, is limited, even though it is a life of comfort, provision, and protection. When birth occurs, the baby continues to experience life, but it is life in a different and fuller form—with almost endless possibilities of fellowship, growth, and activity. As Jesus lives in our hearts now, He provides a new and wonderful quality of life—eternal life; but when we pass over to life's other side, this eternal life will express itself in a different and fuller form—with heavenly fellowship, inexpressible joy, and eternal service.

Christians are part of an eternal kingdom which is not affected by time or physical dimensions. As long as we stay in the sphere of God's protection by faithfulness to His Word, we are part of a kingdom which cannot be destroyed and will never end.

CONCLUSION

Using the rule and reign of God in the heart of the Christian as our frame of reference, the church of the New Testament is the kingdom of God, possessing the traits of spirituality, righteousness, and eternality. Its citizens live in this world, but their hearts and citizenship belong to another world, the eternal kingdom of God (Colossians 3:1, 2; Philippians 3:20).

Nicodemus, a ruler of the Jews, sought Jesus one night to learn more about the kingdom of God. Jesus told him that the kingdom of God can only be entered by a change so radical and transforming that it is best described as a birth. He said, "Truly, truly, I say to you, unless one is born of water and the Spirit, he cannot enter into the kingdom of God" (John 3:5). As the kingdom of God was entered on the day of its official earthly beginning, Peter exhorted the multitude, in light of their faith in Jesus, to repent and be baptized for the forgiveness of their sins (Acts 2:38-41). The new birth which Jesus described to Nicodemus in John 3 was administered by Peter in Acts 2. Entrance or birth into the kingdom of God or the church involves belief in Jesus (John 3:16), repentance or a turning from sin to God (Acts 17:30), acknowledgment of Jesus as God's Son (Romans 10:9, 10), and baptism into Christ for the remission of sins (Acts 2:38; 22:16).

Citizenship in the kingdom of God brings a spiritual center to life, a reign of God, which radiates to every prong and dimension of life, providing stability, guidance, understanding, and wholeness. This holy citizenship also brings righteousness, goodness, and peace into our lives. In this world of the temporary, the kingdom of God infuses eternal life into our lives for today and for all of our tomorrows.

Are you a citizen of God's eternal kingdom, "the church"?

QUESTIONS FOR STUDY AND DISCUSSION

1. List several different traits which the church possesses. Give a brief description of each trait.
2. What verses of Scripture indicate that the church should be viewed as a kingdom?

3. List the different contexts in which the word "kingdom" is used in the New Testament.
4. What conclusions concerning the church does the
   spiritual nature of the kingdom demand? List the
   conclusions and describe them.
5. If we are part of a spiritual kingdom, a new value
   system is imparted to us. Discuss this value system.
6. What two types of righteousness are mentioned in
   the New Testament? Describe each type.
7. Does Daniel 2:44 express the eternal nature of the
   kingdom that God would establish?
8. Discuss how the kingdom of God is an experience
   now and an expectation for the future.
9. Discuss how eternal life is expressed here and how
   it will be expressed in eternity.
10. What implications does our citizenship in heaven
    have on our lives today?
11. How is the kingdom of God entered?
12. Compare John 3:3, 5 with Acts 2:38.

For Preaching and Teaching Purposes: Sermon or Teaching Type:
Basic pattern; deductive; topical. Subject: The church. Theme: The
church, the kingdom of God. Title: The Kingdom of God. Preaching or
Teaching Portion: None. Proposition: (Declarative/didactic) The church
is the kingdom of God on earth. Interrogative Question or Probing
Question: What? Key Word: Characteristics. Major Points: I. A Spiritual Kingdom; II. A Kingdom of Righteousness; III. An Eternal
Kingdom. Sermonic or Teaching Objective: To persuade people to live
as citizens of the kingdom of God.

2

New People in Christ

*"Therefore if any man is in Christ, he is a new
creature; the old things passed away; behold, new
things have come" (2 Corinthians 5:17).*

Everyone enjoys newness. Whether it be a new
baby, a new car, a new house, or just new socks, we are
always thrilled by the freshness and vitality of something new.

The Greek language has two words which are
translated by our single English word "new." One of
the words, *neos*, means "new in time." Using this word,
we could say of a newborn baby, "He is a new human
being." We could use this word to say of a house which
has just been constructed and has never been lived in,
"This is a new house." The baby and the house are truly
"new in time." They have not existed very long.

Another Greek word, *kainos*, basically means "new
in quality." With it, we could say of an old house that
has been renovated, "This is a new house." We could
use it to say of an old car after someone has put a new

motor in it, given it a new set of tires, and painted its body, "This is a new car." The house and car are not "new in time," but they are "new in quality." They have been given new life. They have been remade.

The second word, *kainos*, is the word used by Paul in 2 Corinthians 5:17. Actually, this sentence could be translated, "Therefore if any man is in Christ, he is a new-in-quality person; the old things have passed away; behold, new-in-quality things have come." Paul was not telling us that we can start over again in time, but he was revealing that we can begin anew in quality. He was not giving voice to our wish to recover expended time, as did Elizabeth Akers Allen:

> Backward, turn backward,
> O Time, in your flight,
> Make me a child again just for
> tonight!

Rather, Paul was saying, "Whatever your life has been, it can be made new. If you have been a loser, you can become a winner. If you are spiritually dead, you can be made alive."

The church is the body of people who have been made new through Christ. They are people who have been dead in sin but have been made alive by the gospel. Paul told the church at Colossae, "And when you were dead in your transgressions and the uncircumcision of your flesh, He made you alive together with Him, having forgiven us all our transgressions" (Colossians 2:13). Though Christians have been given new life in Christ, they must be diligent in this new life so that the new life will not be stolen away by sin. Paul exhorted the Ephesians, "In reference to your former manner of life, you lay aside the old self, which is being corrupted in accordance with the lusts of deceit, and . . . you be renewed in the spirit of your mind, and put on the new self, which in the likeness of God has been created in righteousness and holiness of the truth" (Ephesians 4:22-24).

An appropriate question about this new-in-quality life which God gives is this: "How does God give it?" Or, to ask it another way, "What process does God use in order to make us into new creatures in Christ?" This question is answered by Paul in Romans 6.

In Romans 1—3, Paul delineated how people are saved or made righteous before God by obedient faith. In Romans 4 he gave an example of faith making the man, Abraham, righteous before God. Then, in Romans 5—8, Paul enumerated the blessings which accrue from salvation: We have peace with God (5); we are forgiven (6); we are under obedient faith, not under the law of Moses (7); and we have life (8).

In Romans 6, as Paul explained our freedom from sin through Christ, he detailed how God has made us into new people. Come with me to Romans 6, and let us see how God makes us new persons in Christ. The process, as presented by Paul, can be divided into stages. In the growth of a butterfly, scientists have discerned three different stages: the egg stage, the larva stage, and the pupa stage. In a similar way, three stages can be identified in our becoming new people through Christ. If any one of the three stages is omitted, we will abort the process. You can be a new person in Christ; but in order to be completely new you must submit to God's remaking process.

How does God make a new person?

STAGE ONE: SEPARATION

The first stage in the journey to a new life is the separation stage. God's remaking process requires a separation from sin.

Paul wrote, "What shall we say then? Are we to continue in sin that grace might increase? May it never be! How shall we who died to sin still live in it?" (Romans 6:1, 2). Notice carefully the words "died to sin." In the previous chapter, Romans 5, Paul had stressed the grace of God. He had shown that where sin abounds, grace abounds all the more (vv. 20, 21). "God," he said, "overcame our sin problem by His grace, and by this means He has indicated how great He really is." It would be easy for someone to misunderstand this truth. Someone, for example, could say, "Perhaps we should continue in sin that grace may abound. If we have a greater sin problem to overcome, God will have to manifest more grace to save us and by this greater grace He will indicate even better how great He is." Paul anticipated this misunderstanding and raised a question relating to it in the beginning of Romans 6: "Are we to continue in sin that grace might increase?" He answered this question emphatically, saying, "May it never be!" He then asked, "How shall we who died to sin still live in it?" To put it another way, we could say, "It is inappropriate for a Christian to live in sin, because he has died to it."

Our death to sin is not finalized, according to Paul, until we are baptized into Christ. He said in Romans 6:4 that we are baptized into our own spiritual death to sin. However, this baptism into our own death to sin must be preceded by a separation from sin through faith, repentance, and confession of Jesus. Paul did not go into the separation from sin per se in this passage;

he only implied it through his reference to our dying to sin. This separation from sin which is implied by death to sin is affected by faith in God and Christ (Acts 15:9), repentance (1 Thessalonians 1:9), and confession of Jesus as the Christ and Lord (Romans 10:10).

Our death to sin is not finalized,
according to Paul, until we
are baptized into Christ.

Some earlier preachers of the gospel pointed out that three important changes occur as one becomes a Christian. The first change is *a change of heart*, a purification of the heart. This change is produced by faith in Christ. Peter said of the Gentiles, "And He made no distinction between us and them, cleansing their hearts by faith" (Acts 15:9). The second change is *a change in life*, a purging of the life from the practice of sin. Repentance is a change of will which results in a change or reformation of life (Acts 11:18). The third change is *a change of reputation*, a proclaiming of one's belief and allegiance. This change is affected by a confession of Jesus as God's Son and Lord (Romans 10:10). The fourth change is *a change of state*, a placing of one into Christ. This change occurs at baptism (Romans 6:3). The first three of the four changes are implied in Paul's phrase "died to sin," and the fourth change is specifically mentioned in Romans 6:4. According to Paul, complete death to sin has not occurred until all four changes have been experienced.

All of us have known of people who have been baptized by immersion into the name of the Father, the Son, and the Holy Spirit but who, following the baptism, have not exhibited the new life in Christ. After their baptism into Christ, they have continued in their old lives of sin without any change. Looking at their lives, we have probably wondered why they have not entered the new life. Paul gives us at least one answer to this question in Romans 6. He would ask, "Did they separate themselves from sin? Did they completely submit themselves to God's remaking process?" If the separation stage is avoided for whatever reason, one cannot enter the new life in Christ.

Have *you* gone through the separation stage by genuine belief in Christ, repentance of sin, and confession of Jesus as the Christ and Lord?

STAGE TWO: SALVATION

The second stage of God's remaking process we will call the salvation stage. In this stage we are actually brought into the spiritual body of Christ. Uniquely, this stage revolves around baptism.

Paul wrote in Romans 6:3, 4:

> Or do you not know that all of us who have been baptized into Christ Jesus have been baptized into His death? Therefore we have been buried with Him through baptism into death, in order that as Christ was raised from the dead through the glory of the Father, so we too might walk in newness of life.

Where else could we turn in the New Testament and find two verses of Scripture which tell us so much about baptism in so little space? Four significant truths about baptism are *clear* from these two verses.

First, Paul stated that baptism is into Christ: "Or do you not know that all of us who have been baptized into Christ. . . ." (v. 3). In baptism, we are brought by God's grace into the spiritual body of Christ, the church. Baptism is the final part of our faith response to Christ (Galatians 3:26, 27; 2 Timothy 2:10).

Second, Paul said that we are "baptized into His [Christ's] death" (v. 3). In New Testament baptism we are brought into union with the benefits of the death of Christ. Whatever Jesus made available to us in His death, we receive in baptism.

Third, Paul affirmed that we are buried in baptism: "Therefore we have been buried with Him through baptism. . . ." (v. 4). New Testament baptism is a burial or an immersion. This Greek word *baptizo* in most of our translations has not been translated—it has been transliterated. In transliteration, the Greek word is Anglicized, or converted to an English word. In translation, the corresponding English word is used for the Greek word being translated. According to Greek scholars, the corresponding English word for *baptizo* is "immerse." This definition of *baptizo* is confirmed by the way Paul used the word in this verse (and in Colossians 2:12). We can be certain that New Testament baptism is a burial or an immersion.

Fourth, Paul wrote that we are baptized into our own spiritual death to sin. He said, "Therefore we have been buried with Him through baptism into death, in order that as Christ was raised from the dead through the glory of the Father, so we too might walk in newness of life" (v. 4). Our death to sin is finalized in baptism. Through faith, repentance, confession of Jesus, and baptism, our "old self was crucified with Him, that our body of sin might be done away with, that we should no longer be slaves to sin; for he who has died is freed from sin" (Romans 6:6, 7).

One of the momentous events in the life of Christ was His baptism by John. His earthly ministry is prefaced with His baptism and His temptations. When Jesus appeared on the shore of the Jordan River and waded out to John to be baptized of him, John was hesitant to baptize Him and said, "I have need to be baptized by You, and do You come to me?" (Matthew 3:14). Jesus said, "Permit it at this time; for in this way it is fitting for us to fulfill all righteousness" (Matthew 3:15). When Jesus was raised up out of the water from the baptism, two significant events took place. His Father in heaven publicly acknowledged Him as His Son for the first time, with the words, "This is My beloved Son, in whom I am well-pleased" (Matthew 3:17), and the Holy Spirit descended upon Him in the form of a dove (Matthew 3:16). John had been told that the One upon whom the Spirit descended and remained was the Son of God (John 1:33). From the baptism of Jesus forward, therefore, John testified to His deity (John 1:29). The baptism of Jesus marked the beginning of His ministry.

The significance of Jesus' baptism reminds us of the significance of our baptism. Consider how momentous our baptism is. According to Paul, we are baptized or buried into Christ and into His body, the church. We are brought into union with His death and the benefits of His death. We are baptized into our own spiritual death to sin, as the old man of sin is being separated from us and we are being raised to walk in newness of life.

Have *you* passed through this stage of God's remaking process? Have *you* been baptized into Christ, into His death, and into your own spiritual death to sin?

STAGE THREE: STAY-WITH-IT

The third stage of God's remarkable remaking process might be called the stay-with-it stage. Once we are remade, we must stay remade. God can give us the new life, but we must live it. He can put us on the S & N Road, the straight and narrow road, but we have to stay on it.

In the remaining verses of Romans 6, Paul listed at least four characteristics of the new life we have in Christ. Each of the traits of the new life must be maintained daily.

First, Paul said that in Christ we have a new freedom—we are free from sin. "For he who has died is freed from sin" (Romans 6:7). Freedom is a generic term and must be given a specific context before it has real meaning. When someone says, "I'd like to be free," I want to ask, "Free from what?" One cannot be just free. Does he want to be free from working? Free from rules? Free from sleeping? One has to be free *from* something. Paul gave the words "free," "freed," and "freedom" a context in Romans 6. He said that in Christ we are free from sin—free from its guilt (Romans 3:24; 6:3); free from its grip (Romans 6:17); and free from its grave, or condemnation (Romans 6:21).

Second, Paul mentioned that the new life is characterized by a new fellowship—we have fellowship with God. "Even so consider yourselves to be dead to sin, but alive to God in Christ Jesus," he said (Romans 6:11). Two contrasts are seen in this verse; one is implied, and the other is expressed. The implied truth says that before you became a Christian, you were dead toward God but alive toward sin. The expressed contrast says that as a Christian you are alive toward God and dead toward sin. In Christ, you have come into a new fellowship, a new relationship with God. You have a heavenly Father to pray to and a loving Savior to pray through. You are alive toward God's existence, fellowship, blessings, promises, and the spiritual life which He gives.

Third, Paul explained that the new life in Christ is characterized by a new fruitfulness.

> Therefore what benefit [fruit] were you then deriving from the things of which you are now ashamed? For the outcome of those things is death. But now having been freed from sin and enslaved to God, you derive your benefit [fruit], resulting in sanctification, and the outcome, eternal life (Romans 6:21, 22).

The non-Christian brings forth a kind of fruit, but not a lasting, beneficial fruit—"for the outcome of those things is death." The Christian brings forth a fruit that endures when life's little day has passed. He produces the spiritual fruit of Christian character and the "forever" fruit of eternal life. Someone has said, "Only what we give to God do we get to keep." We invest our lives in Christ's life and work, and He brings forth from that investment the imperishable fruit of Christian character and eternal life.

Fourth, Paul said the new life in Christ is characterized by a new future: "For the wages of sin is death, but the free gift of God is eternal life in Christ Jesus our Lord" (Romans 6:23). The Christian is on his way to heaven. He has read the last chapter in the book of life, the Bible, and he knows that the Lord's side wins. He may struggle in this world, becoming bruised and lacerated at times, but he knows the ultimate victory is his!

The new life in Christ is attractive to anyone who has an honest heart and wants to live a good life. A new life is ours when we become Christians—a life of freedom from sin, a life of fellowship with Him, a life of fruitfulness, and a life with an eternal future in heaven.

The new life must be preserved and maintained. Suppose you were given a new car to own, drive, and enjoy. You would have the responsibility to maintain it if you wanted to enjoy it for a while. If you did not drive it carefully, take care of its engine, keep air in its tires, and provide it with gasoline, the car would not be yours to use very long.

A Christian has to guard his freedom from sin. He must keep his mind clean and not allow evil to return to dominate his life. He must cultivate his fellowship with God through prayer, Bible study, fellowship with other Christians, and a daily walk with God. He must continue producing fruit by striving to grow, by seeking to lead others to Christ, and by building character in himself and others. He must affirm his hope of eternal life by keeping this hope burning brightly in his heart.

CONCLUSION

You can be a new person in Christ today. God asks you through His Word to submit to His remaking process so that He can remake you and give you His new life in Christ. His process involves separation, salvation, and staying with it. Each stage is significant and essential.

Just think of what it would be like to have this new life in Christ! After being away from home for a couple of days, suppose you returned home and discovered that everything in your house was brand new, that someone had come into your house while you were gone and had made everything new. What would you do? Perhaps you would run through the house checking out everything. You would see new chairs, new tables, new beds, new towels, new clothes, new shoes, new appliances, new carpets and rugs, and many other new things. Would you not be thrilled at all of your new possessions? Surely you would be overwhelmed with delight and excitement!

Most likely, an experience of this kind will never happen to you or me. The possibility is extremely slim that you will ever go home and find that someone has replaced everything in your house with brand new furniture and clothes. Something else is possible and is far greater than having all new possessions: You can be a new person. You can be remade through God's divine process today.

The church is made up of the people who have received God's new life. They are the new-life family. At the same time that God makes you into a new person, He puts you in His church. Why not enter the company of the new life by submitting to God's remaking process today?

QUESTIONS FOR STUDY
AND DISCUSSION

1. What is the difference between the Greek words *neos* and *kainos*? Apply this difference to 2 Corinthians 5:17.
2. In what sense were we dead before we became Christians?
3. Give a brief outline of Romans 1—8.

4. Tell what Paul meant by the question "Are we to continue in sin that grace might increase?" (Romans 6:1).
5. When or at what point is our death to sin finalized?
6. How is separation from sin brought about in the conversion process?
7. What would be true of one's conversion if the separation stage were omitted?
8. How are we brought into Christ?
9. What is the meaning of the Greek word *baptizo*?
10. What did Paul mean when he said that we are baptized into death in Romans 6:4?
11. List the four characteristics of baptism which Paul mentioned in Romans 6:1-4.
12. What kind of freedom are we granted in Christ, according to Romans 6:7?
13. What did Paul mean when he referred to being "alive to God"?
14. What kind of fruit does a Christian bring forth?
15. What future does the Christian have? Describe it.

For Preaching and Teaching Purposes: Sermon or Teaching Type: Basic pattern; deductive; expository. Subject: Conversion. Theme: How God makes us new creatures. Title: New People in Christ. Preaching or Teaching Portion: Romans 6. Proposition: (Declarative/sermonic) You can be a new creature in Christ. Interrogative Question or Probing Question: How? Key Word: Stages. Major Points: I. Stage One: Separation; II. Stage Two: Salvation; III. Stage Three: Stay-With-It. Sermonic or Teaching Objective: To persuade people to become new creatures in Christ.

3

Living in Christ

"Blessed be the God and Father of our Lord Jesus Christ, who has blessed us with every spiritual blessing in the heavenly places in Christ" (Ephesians 1:3).

In many cultures of the world the wearing of a wedding ring symbolizes the commitment of a man and a woman to each other in marriage. The visible sign of this commitment is small (and most often expensive), but the meaning of it signifies a lifelong promise. This tiny symbol of marriage reminds us that small items often convey extremely important ideas.

The New Testament phrase "in Christ," a two-word phrase which is at times almost inconspicuous, is always very meaningful. It never appears without carrying a weighty spiritual concept. It may be worded "in Christ" (Romans 12:5), "in Christ Jesus" (Romans 3:24), "in Christ Jesus our Lord" (Romans 8:39), "in Him" (2 Corinthians 5:21), "in the Lord Jesus" (Romans 14:14), "in the Lord" (1 Corinthians 4:17), "in His Son" (1 John 5:11), "in Jesus" (Ephesians 4:21), "into

Him" (Ephesians 4:15), "in whom" (Ephesians 2:21), "in the Lord Jesus Christ" (2 Thessalonians 3:12), "in Jesus" (1 Thessalonians 4:14), or "in His Son Jesus Christ" (1 John 5:20); but its theological connotations cannot be overlooked. It suggests a union with Christ, an abiding in the spiritual body of Christ. We cannot, therefore, understand the meaning and place of the church in God's plan if we ignore the implications of this phrase.

The two phrases "in Christ" and "in the church" have essentially the same meaning in the writings of the New Testament. As Paul wrote of the exaltation of Jesus, affirming that all things have been placed under His feet and that He has become head over all things "to the church," he said that the church is "His body, the fulness of Him who fills all in all" (Ephesians 1:22, 23). According to Paul, the church is the body of Christ; thus, to be "in Christ" is to be in Christ's church.

When we trace this phrase "in Christ" or its equivalents through the New Testament (especially in the writings of Paul), we see the breathtaking theological meaning of the church and *our* relation to it.[1] Careful consideration of it impresses us with the grandeur of the spiritual blessings which are ours in His body. Without an understanding of this phrase, we cannot hope to have the scriptural view of what it means to be a member of Christ's church.

A PLACE OF PRIVILEGE

First, the phrase "in Christ" suggests the privilege

---

[1] Appendix 3 includes all appearances of the phrase "in Christ" and its equivalents in the New Testament. This list will allow you the opportunity to study carefully the use of this phrase and to consider its tremendous implications for the meaning of the church.

that belongs to those who are members of the Lord's church. "In Christ" we are the chosen of God.

In the extended doxology of Ephesians 1:3-14, Paul praised God for making those "in Christ" His chosen ones:

> Just as He chose us in Him before the foundation of the world, that we should be holy and blameless before Him. In love He predestined us to adoption as sons through Jesus Christ to Himself, according to the kind intention of His will, to the praise of the glory of His grace, which He freely bestowed on us in the Beloved" (Ephesians 1:4-6).

Paul was not writing of a predestination of individuals, a choosing of one to be saved and another to be lost. He was pointing to God's wonderful pre-determined choice to save all who come into Christ and faithfully abide in Him. Before the foundation of the world, God chose that the body of Christ would be the place of privilege, choosing to adopt as His children those who come into the body of Christ.

This divine choice does not conflict with man's freedom of choice. Rather, it gives man the freedom to choose to be among the chosen. God has already chosen to save the body of Christ; but man must choose to come into that body, and he must choose to remain in it.

God chose a place for Noah to be saved (Genesis 7:1), but Noah and his family had to enter it and stay in it (Genesis 7:7). The ark was the place of privilege for Noah and his family. Of all the peoples of the earth, Noah and his wife, sons, and daughters-in-law who were *in the ark* were God's chosen people—they were protected and provided for by God's grace and care.

Someone has said that when *we* get to heaven we will see a large, billboard-like sign next to the entrance to heaven. On the front side of the billboard will be the words "Come Unto Me." As we enter heaven, we will read those words and think of the Lord's invitation to come to Him for salvation and the choice God gave each man to answer that invitation. After entering heaven, we will turn to read the back side of the billboard. It will read: "Chosen of God." Then we will think of the choice God made before the creation of the world to save the body of Christ and of the incomparable privilege which God bestowed upon all who entered and remained in that body.

Anyone who enters the body of Christ, the church, enters into the place of privilege, the place of divine choice. Whether or not we are God's children is not a matter of chance, but a matter of choice. God has chosen the place of salvation, but we must choose to enter into that place and to stay in it. When we choose to enter into the body of Christ, God chooses us to be His children and heirs according to His promises.

A PLACE OF PROVISION

In addition to his being in a place of privilege, the person "in Christ" has access to all of the abundant spiritual provisions of God. Paul wrote that the body of Christ is "the fulness of Him who fills all in all" (Ephesians 1:23). He further said, "For it was the Father's good pleasure for all the fulness to dwell in Him" (Colossians 1:19). Hence, he could say, "In Him you have been made complete" (Colossians 2:10).

Every spiritual blessing which God provides for us is found "in Christ." As Paul began his doxology in

Ephesians 1, he summarized what God has done for us in Christ with one sweeping sentence: "Blessed be the God and Father of our Lord Jesus Christ, who has blessed us with every spiritual blessing in the heavenly places in Christ" (Ephesians 1:3). Paul's "every" is exhaustive. No person, however, can receive God's bounteous, lavish spiritual provisions except by coming into Christ and abiding in Him.

Every spiritual blessing
which God provides for us
is found "in Christ."

Think of the blessings that are accessible to us "in Christ." First, we have blessings regarding *salvation* "in Christ." "In Him" we have forgiveness: "In Him we have redemption through His blood, the forgiveness of our trespasses, according to the riches of His grace" (Ephesians 1:7). "In Christ" we are a new creation: "Therefore if any man is in Christ, he is a new creature; the old things passed away; behold, new things have come" (2 Corinthians 5:17). "In Jesus Christ" we have eternal life: "For this reason I endure all things for the sake of those who are chosen, that they also may obtain the salvation which is in Christ Jesus and with it eternal glory" (2 Timothy 2:10).

Second, we have blessings regarding *sonship* "in Christ." "In Christ Jesus" we have full access to the Father: "But now in Christ Jesus you who formerly were far off have been brought near by the blood of Christ"; "For through Him we both have our access in one Spirit to the Father" (Ephesians 2:13, 18). "In Him" we have an eternal inheritance: ". . . in Him also we have obtained an inheritance, having been predestined according to His purpose who works all things after the counsel of His will" (Ephesians 1:10, 11).

Third, we have blessings concerning *security* "in Christ." "In Him" we are sealed with the Holy Spirit: "In Him, you also, after listening to the message of truth, the gospel of your salvation—having also believed, you were sealed in Him with the Holy Spirit of promise" (Ephesians 1:13). "In Christ" we are free from condemnation: "There is therefore now no condemnation for those who are in Christ Jesus" (Romans 8:1).

Our Father in heaven has chosen the body of Christ to be the place of all spiritual blessings. Only those who enter that body and abide in it have access to His generous bounties.

Consider this Old Testament example. Israel is preparing to leave Egypt and journey to the promised land of Canaan. The first Passover is taking place. God has instructed the Israelites to place blood from the Passover lamb on the top and the sides of the doors of their houses and during the evening of the Passover to remain in their houses (Exodus 12:22). Those who do not carry out this instruction will lose their first-born by death when God passes over. How solemn that approaching historic evening will be! Every Israelite family will be staying up all night in a solemn vigil. Shortly before the evening begins, we can imagine an eldest son asking his father, "Father, are you sure the blood has been placed on the doorposts and lintel?" The father responds, "Yes, my son. I did it myself. It has been done." A little later, the son asks again, "Father, don't you think we should check to make sure you did it right? The evening is about to begin, and we will have to remain inside our house and will not be able to check it anymore." The father says, "All right. I will check and make sure everything has been done properly." The father checks and affirms that he has put the blood on the doorposts and lintel as God instructed. The father returns to comfort his son with this assurance: "All is well, my son. We have followed God's instructions. You are safe in God's will."

That father could assure his son because they were living within the circle of God's instructions. Likewise, "in Christ" we are within the sphere of God's will. Our Father will meet all of our spiritual needs as long as we faithfully abide in His Son.

A PLACE OF PROMISE

Third, our only hope for the future is "in Christ." Human wisdom fails as a true, unerring guide for this life, but in Christ are "hidden all the treasures of wisdom and knowledge" (Colossians 2:3). This world is destined for destruction (2 Peter 3:10). Any hope, therefore, based upon this world will eventually perish, but "in Christ" we have an eternal, unfading inheritance (Ephesians 1:11).

Concerning our hope in Christ, John wrote, "And the witness is this, that God has given us eternal life, and this life is in His Son" (1 John 5:11). This eternal life comes to us in two ways: as abundant life in this world and as eternal life in the world to come. In Christ we have hope in this life and hope for the life to come— abundant life now and eternal life in heaven. Jesus said, "I came that they might have life, and might have it abundantly" (John 10:10). John further said, "He who has the Son has the life; he who does not have the Son of God does not have the life" (1 John 5:12). Still further John wrote, "These things I have written to you who believe in the name of the Son of God, in order that you may know that you have eternal life" (1 John 5:13).

Under Old Testament law, a man who had accidentally killed someone could flee to a city of refuge for protection from the man known as "the avenger of blood," who would be seeking to avenge the death of his relative (Joshua 20). As long as he stayed within the city of refuge, he was protected. In that city he could have a normal life and a normal future. If he left the city, he would be constantly pursued by the avenger of blood and most likely would be killed by him. He had a life and a future only in the city of refuge.

Likewise, our only hope is "in Christ." Outside of Him we do not have the provisions we need for an abundant life in this world or the secure hope for eternity. Paul says that the Gentiles who were separated from Christ were without hope in the world (Ephesians 2:12). Likewise, anyone who is outside of Christ is without hope in this world.

CONCLUSION

In light of the significance of the phrase "in Christ," we would be foolish not to ask, "How can we come into Christ?" Two passages answer our question. First, Paul said in Romans 6:3 that we are brought into Christ through New Testament baptism: "Or do you not know that all of us who have been baptized into Christ Jesus have been baptized into His death?" Second, Paul gave us the same truth in Galatians 3:27: "For all of you who were baptized into Christ have clothed yourselves with Christ."

When we believe in Christ, repent of the life of sin and turn to God, confess that Jesus is the Christ, and are baptized for the remission of sins, we are brought into Christ by the gracious action of God. Our *position* is immediately changed, for we have been brought into a place of privilege, provision, and promise. Our *condition* will continually change as we grow day by day through feeding on the Word of God, fellowship with Christ and the family of God, and walking in the light.

I have read of a denominational church which discovered oil on its property. It was a gusher, and the church had suddenly become rich. They immediately closed their membership and decided to divide up the monthly profits equally among the members. This church suddenly became a business and brought great material riches to those in it.

The church of the New Testament is so different from this denomination and all other denominations! It is the spiritual body of Christ, filled with the riches of heaven. The membership is never closed. Anyone who will obey the gospel can enter it and partake of God's bounties. Each member has free access by the Spirit through Jesus to all spiritual blessings at all times. No one will ever find heaven's bank closed or unable to provide an inexhaustible supply of spiritual treasures.

Since the person in Christ has the privilege of being God's child, has all spiritual blessings, and has the hope of eternal life, surely no greater question could be asked of us than the question "Are you in Christ?"

QUESTIONS FOR STUDY
AND DISCUSSION

1. List different ways that the phrase "in Christ" appears in the New Testament.
2. Compare the phrases "in Christ" and "in the church."
3. Describe the predestination of which Paul wrote in Ephesians 1:4-6.
4. Relate the concept of predestination to Noah and his family and the flood.
5. List some of the key blessings we have "in Christ," and describe each one briefly.
6. Relate "abundant life" to "eternal life."
7. Describe the cities of refuge and their function in the Old Testament era.
8. Describe Ephesians 2:12 in connection with being "in Christ."
9. What does Romans 6:3 say about entrance into Christ?
10. What does Galatians 3:27 say about entrance into Christ?
11. Compare our *position* in Christ with our *condition* in Christ.
12. How can we be assured that we are "in Christ"?

For Preaching and Teaching Purposes: Sermon or Teaching Type: Basic pattern; deductive; topical. Subject: The church. Theme: The church, being in Christ. Title: Living in Christ. Preaching or Teaching Portion: None. Proposition: (Evaluative) In Christ is the best place to be. Interrogative Question or Probing Question: Why? Key Word: Reasons. Major Points: I. A Place of Privilege; II. A Place of Provisions; III. A Place of Promise. Sermonic or Teaching Objective: (Evangelistic) To motivate non-Christians to come into Christ.

4

The Body of Christ

"Now you are Christ's body, and individually members of it" (1 Corinthians 12:27).

Suppose a man attempted to use a small airplane as a car. He would find the airplane hard to steer, awkward to turn at corners, abnormal for passenger comfort, improperly designed for land travel, and completely unsuited for highway traffic. To designate an airplane as appropriate for use as a car is unrealistic because of the "intrinsic character" of the airplane. It was not built for this use, and such a use of it would violate its nature.

Erroneous pictures of the church of the New Testament are often held because the church's nature is misunderstood. Therefore, acquiring an understanding of the "intrinsic character" of the church is necessary for perceiving accurately its function, purpose, and identity in the world.

As we have seen, one of the key expressions in the New Testament (especially in the writings of Paul) for the church is "the body of Christ."[1] This phrase is used both as a practical illustration of the church (1 Corinthians 12:23-26) and as a functional description of the church (1 Corinthians 12:27). The nature of the New Testament church cannot be understood unless this phrase as a description of the church is comprehended.

Let us give special attention to this New Testament designation for the church. What does this expression convey?

UNION WITH CHRIST

First, this phrase indicates union with Christ. Conversion is more than "the pledging of one's loyalty to Christ." It is being uniquely united with Christ as one enters the spiritual body of Christ.

As part of the process of conversion to Christ, we are baptized into Christ. Paul wrote, "Or do you not know that all of us who have been baptized into Christ Jesus have been baptized into His death?" (Romans 6:3). The idea of being united with Christ is especially observed in Romans 6:4: "Therefore we have been buried *with Him* through baptism into death, in order that as Christ was raised from the dead through the glory of the Father, so we too might walk in newness of life." (Emphasis mine.) Paul also said, "For by one Spirit we were all baptized into one body, . . ." (1 Corinthians 12:13). At baptism, then, we are brought into union with Christ as we are implanted into His spiritual body.

---

[1]Appendix 3 includes all appearances of the phrase "the body of Christ" in the New Testament. This list will help you to study the use of this phrase and to consider this important aspect of the nature of the church.

This singular, spiritual union with Christ might be compared to marriage. When a man and a woman enter into marriage, more is taking place than "two people making a commitment to each other for life." In marriage, a union occurs—a union so profound that the husband and wife can be referred to as "one flesh" for life (Ephesians 5:31). We often say of a couple, "They said their vows to each other." Perhaps it would be better to say, "They entered into the union of marriage." The word "union" conveys a continual oneness. Marriage does not consist of two just agreeing to walk together or to live in the same house; marriage is an agreement of two to be one for life, to be joined together in a marital union that only fornication or death can destroy. This is true to the extent that when two enter marriage they surrender authority over even their own bodies. Paul wrote, "The wife does not have authority over her own body, but the husband does; and likewise also the husband does not have authority over his own body, but the wife does" (1 Corinthians 7:4).

In like manner, at conversion we enter into a union with Christ as we are added to His spiritual body, the church. We become one with Christ—Christ is ours and we are Christ's. No longer do we have authority over our own lives; we belong to Christ—we live in perpetual oneness with Him (1 Corinthians 6:16).

UNITY THROUGH CHRIST

Second, the description of the church as the "body of Christ" suggests unity through Christ. It pictures the church as an organism with many members functioning together as one body.

Paul wrote, "For even as the body is one and yet has

many members, and all the members of the body, though they are many, are one body, so also is Christ" (1 Corinthians 12:12). Many different members comprise the one body of Christ. What Paul said of the physical body could be said of the church: "For the body is not one member, but many"; "And if they were all one member, where would the body be?" (1 Corinthians 12:14, 19). Thus, it must be concluded that Christians "are Christ's body, and individually members of it" (1 Corinthians 12:27).

The unity experienced by the members of the body of Christ should be similar to the unity of the members of the physical body.

The expression "body of Christ" not only suggests that we belong to Christ but that we also belong to each other as each member of a physical body belongs to the other members. When one member of the body hurts, all the members sympathize and hurt. An obvious deduction from the "body" concept would be this: "That there should be no division in the body, but that the members should have the same care for one another. And if one member suffers, all the members suffer with it; if one member is honored, all the members rejoice with it" (1 Corinthians 12:25, 26).

When the expression "body of Christ" is understood, the rationale for denominationalism is destroyed. Denominationalism advocates many different bodies, each having different identities and beliefs. The "body of Christ" concept of the New Testament pictures one body, the body of Christ, with every Christian as a member of it, loving all other members and looking out for every other member of that body. If the church of the New Testament is the body of Christ, denominationalism cannot be God's design for "the church"; if denominationalism is right, the New Testament church cannot be the one body of Christ.

On the night of His betrayal and arrest, Jesus prayed for the unity of those who would later believe on Him (John 17:21-24). On Pentecost, after His resurrection from the dead, He established the church which, as His earthly body, would create and maintain that unity for which He had prayed. As we enter the body of Christ, we enter into a unity with all the members of that body. All dividing walls are broken down: "There is neither Jew nor Greek, there is neither slave nor free man, there is neither male nor female; for you are all one in Christ Jesus" (Galatians 3:28).

The unity experienced by the members of the body of Christ should be similar to the unity of the members of the physical body—the unity of working together, loving each other, and sympathizing with each other. No one member of a physical body is in competition with any other member. Each member works with all other members and produces a coordinated entity which functions as a united body.

The only request Jesus has ever made of His people is that they be His spiritual body on the earth. He did not asked them to be denominations of all types and names. Loyalty to Him demands that we honor Him by fulfilling His request to be His one spiritual body.

UTILITY FOR CHRIST

Third, the "body" description of the church connotes utility or usefulness for Christ. It implies the way

Christ's work is to be done in the world.

Of his life and service, Paul could say, "For to me, to live is Christ, . . ." (Philippians 1:21). He did not represent a denomination or any other manmade group or organization; he stood before men as a member of the spiritual body of Christ. He saw himself as God's instrument of reconciliation among men: "Therefore, we are ambassadors for Christ, as though God were entreating through us; we beg you on behalf of Christ, be reconciled to God" (2 Corinthians 5:20). Paul even saw his sufferings as being for Christ's body: "Now I rejoice in my sufferings for your sake, and in my flesh I do my share on behalf of His body (which is the church) in filling up that which is lacking in Christ's afflictions" (Colossians 1:24).

How is the work of Christ to be carried out on earth? How is the earthly ministry to be continued now that Christ is at the Father's right hand in heaven? The answer to these questions is plainly "through the body of Christ." With the establishment of the church, Jesus sent forth into the world His spiritual body as His means of serving and loving the world.

The New Testament does not speak of a headless body or a bodiless head. If no Christians existed on the earth, Christ would have no body to guide, to direct, or to do His work. If Christians did not look to Christ as their sole authority and guide, the church would be a headless body. Jesus is the head of His church, and His church is made up of the people on the earth who have yielded to His will and who function as His work force here.

Christians are Christ's spiritual body to do His work. We are His eyes to see the needs of the world. If we do not see human need and minister to it, the eyes of His spiritual body are sightless eyes. We are His ears to hear His Word and heed His directions. How tragic it would be if Christ's spiritual body were deaf to His will! We are His tongue to speak His Word and to sing His praises in the world. It would indeed be heart-breaking to Christ if His body were to be speechless at such a time as this. We are His shoulders to carry burdens and responsibilities. Christ wants His church to be healthy and strong so that we can carry whatever assignments He may give us. We are His feet to run His errands in the world. We must keep His feet strong and make them swift to run for Him. We are to be His gentle hands of service. Let us make sure that His hands are complete, competent, and committed for service.

Think of the utility, the genius, and the practicality of the spiritual body of Christ. Anytime, anywhere someone becomes a Christian, he becomes a functioning member of Christ's body to do His work and to manifest His love. By this means, he continues to carry on the ministry of Christ. He is one with Christ and one with all other members of His body. Thus, the unity of Christ's church is evident to the world. Each Christian refers to himself only in the way the Bible refers to the church. He does not look to any earthly headquarters for his guidance; he looks only to Christ, the head of the body. As a result, all honor and glory is given to Christ. See how simple, yet how wise and effective, the "body of Christ" is!

Even to our finite human wisdom, the "body of Christ" concept makes sense. It is efficient, workable, and practical. It reflects God's wisdom and glory.

Let us do the work of Christ as the body of Christ for the glory of Christ.

CONCLUSION

The church is the body of Christ on the earth. Because of this truth, Paul said of the Christians in Rome, "For just as we have many members in one body and all the members do not have the same function, so we, who are many, are one body in Christ, and individually members one of another" (Romans 12:4, 5). In becoming Christians, we enter into a union with Christ, a unity with each other through Christ, and a utility, a usefulness, for Christ.

What a difference exists between a mannequin in a department store window and a human being! The mannequin has form but no life. It has an outside, a body, but no inside, no spirit. It is just a replica, an artificial representation, not the real thing. A human being has form, spirit, and life; he is genuine in body and spirit. He has a body, a soul, and a mind. He can think, feel, love, and obey.

The difference between a mannequin and a human being illustrates the difference between a manmade organization and the body of Christ. The human organization has form, but God does not indwell it; only man dwells within it. Whatever a human organization seeks to accomplish must be done through the energy and wisdom of man alone. The body of Christ is indwelt by the Spirit, is alive with the life of God, and is guided and directed by Christ Himself.

The church of the New Testament is the body of Christ. Every authentic Christian is a member of it. It is not an organization, but an organism which is alive with the Spirit of Christ. It is guided by Christ, its head. Its purpose in the world is to live and serve to the glory of Christ.

Are you a member of the body of Christ?

QUESTIONS FOR STUDY
AND DISCUSSION

1. Discuss the two ways the phrase "the body of Christ" is used in connection with the church.
2. Describe our baptism into Christ in terms of being united with Christ.
3. What does Romans 6:3 say about coming into Christ?
4. Compare our union with Christ with oneness in marriage.
5. What does Romans 6:4 say about union with Christ?
6. How does 1 Corinthians 12:13 say we enter Christ?
7. Who are the members of the body of Christ, churches or Christians?
8. What does the phrase "the body of Christ" suggest concerning our relationship with one another?
9. Discuss denominationalism in connection with the unity concept of the body of Christ.
10. What does Galatians 3:28 say about our unity in Christ?
11. In what way is the work of Christ to be done in the world?
12. Is the church a headless body or a bodiless head?
13. How do we function as the body of Christ in the world?
14. Are the church and "the body of Christ" the same?
15. Compare and contrast an organization and an organism.

For Preaching and Teaching Purposes: Sermon or Teaching Type: Basic pattern; deductive; topical. Subject: The church. Theme: The church, the body of Christ. Title: The Body of Christ. Preaching or Teaching Portion: None; topical. Proposition: (Declarative/didactic)

The church is the body of Christ. Interrogative Question or Probing Question: What? Key Word: Characteristics. Major Points: I. Union With Christ; II. Unity Through Christ; III. Utility for Christ. Sermonic or Teaching Objective: To persuade people to live as members of the body of Christ.

5

The Elect of God

"Just as He chose us in Him before the foundation of the world, that we should be holy and blameless before Him. In love He predestined us to adoption as sons through Jesus Christ to Himself, according to the kind intention of His will, to the praise of the glory of His grace, which He freely bestowed on us in the Beloved" (Ephesians 1:4-6).

Everyone likes to be remembered. Perhaps this desire in all of us is what has given rise to some of our popular colloquial expressions. We write across a birthday card we are sending to a loved one, "I'm thinking of you." In a telephone conversation, we say to a friend whose companionship has been especially dear to us, "I've been thinking of you." As we say good-by to home folks when we leave on a vacation or on another trip, we say, "We'll be thinking about you." These are tender expressions which convey that a person is special and has not been or will not be forgotten. When sincerely spoken or written to us, these expressions touch and encourage us.

If it is meaningful to us to hear friends and relatives say that they are or have been thinking of us, how much more meaningful it is to hear God say that we are special in His sight! If you are in Christ, God has said this very thing to you. Paul said in Ephesians 1:4-6 that Christians are the chosen of God. All redeemed ones in Christ are assured by the Scriptures that they are the elect of God! Does this not greatly encourage you?

We know from the way Paul worded this sentence that the Spirit meant for us to see being chosen of God as something very important, something greater than any earthly honor. Paul was writing to the church in Ephesus in Asia Minor. The theme for his epistle could be summarized with the phrase "the church, the body of Christ." Paul wrote at the beginning of the letter that the church is made up of the ones whom God has chosen. They are the elect of God, the ones whom He has selected for His divine blessings. He calls this type of choosing "predestination," a determining before-hand or a choosing in advance (Ephesians 1:5).

This matter of God's choosing us raises some questions, does it not? Was Paul saying that God chooses one person to be saved and another to be lost? How could God have a special love for each person of the world, as Jesus said in John 3:16, if He chooses one for heaven and another for hell?

Let us give careful thought to this passage and allow Paul to answer our questions on this fascinating subject of predestination. In Ephesians 1:4-6, we will see how God loves everyone, how He thought of us before the foundation of the world, and how He chose to have chosen ones.

CHOSEN IN HIM

First, Paul said that God "chose us *in Him. . . .*" (Ephesians 1:4; emphasis mine). The body of His Son is the place where God has chosen to offer to man His salvation and His other spiritual blessings. Those who have come into this body are the chosen of God.

In the larger context of Ephesians 1:4-6, the entire doxology of 1:3-14, which is said to be the longest sentence in the Bible, Paul enumerates specific blessings which God has placed in Christ. He mentions adoption as God's children (v. 5), forgiveness (v. 7), redemption (v. 7), wisdom and insight (v. 8), a summing up in Christ (v. 10), an inheritance (v. 11), and the sealing of the Holy Spirit (v. 13).

God, in ageless eternity past, decided that those who would come into Christ and would avail themselves of Christ's gift of grace would be His chosen ones, chosen for His blessings and His salvation. This plan of salvation was predestined, determined beforehand, by God in eternity past. He was not capricious or partial in His choosing. He did not predestine one person to be lost and another person to be saved, but He did determine that the only ones He would save would be those who receive the salvation of Christ by entering His spiritual body, the church.

The word "predestine" means "to fix before," whereas "foreknowledge" means "to know before." Perhaps God foreknows who will be saved and who will be lost, but He does not predestine their personal salvation or their personal destruction. Each person chooses whether or not he will be saved by what he decides to do about coming into Christ.

These two subjects, foreknowledge and predestination, are obviously too deep for us to understand completely. To some degree, we will just have to accept by faith what the Bible says concerning them. The Bible does imply, though, that God can foreknow without predestining. The foreknowledge of God has been likened to our memory. We can remember what happened yesterday, but our remembering the events of yesterday does not cause them to happen. Perhaps the foreknowledge of God goes forward in time somewhat the way our memories go backward in time. God may see the future in His foreknowledge even as we see the past in our memory. In His omniscience, He sees the future; but His seeing it does not make the events of the future happen.

Both concepts of free moral choice and predestination are found in the New Testament in one verse, Acts 2:23. They are used in the same sentence and do not contradict each other. Peter said, "This Man, delivered up by the predetermined plan and foreknowledge of God, you nailed to a cross by the hands of godless men and put Him to death" (Acts 2:23). God foreknew the death of Jesus; He even predetermined it or predestined it, but He held responsible the godless men who did it. The free moral choice of man and foreknowledge and predestination by God are found in this one verse, yet one concept does not cancel out the other.

God planned or predestined our salvation in Christ before the foundation of the world, but we must choose to come into the sphere of salvation, the body of Christ, to be saved. Anyone can choose to be among the chosen of God. Someone has said, "The whosoever-will's are the elect, and the whosoever-won'ts are the non-elect."

Have you been chosen of God? How can you know that you have been chosen of Him? According to Paul, the answer is simple: Are you in Him? Those who are in Christ can rejoice that they are among the chosen. In Christ we are in the place of blessing which God chose or predestined in dateless eternity past. If we faithfully live in Christ during our time on the earth, heaven will be our eternal inheritance.

CHOSEN FROM ETERNITY

Second, Paul said that the elect ones of God, the church, were chosen from eternity, chosen before the foundation of the world. His words are, ". . . He chose us in Him *before the foundation of the world,...*" (Ephesians 1:4; emphasis mine).

Paul used a very basic Greek word which has been translated "foundation" in the NASB. It actually means "before the beginning of the beginning." God first thought of us, picked us out to be His peculiar people, in beginningless eternity past before we sinned, before we were created, and before the world was made. In His holy and infinite mind, He chose us to be His elect people by devising a plan of salvation which centered in Jesus, His death on the cross, and the spiritual body of Christ, the church. In this sense, Jesus can be spoken of as the Lamb of God who was slain from the foundation of the world (Revelation 13:8; 1 Peter 1:19, 20).

God told Jeremiah, "Before I formed you in the womb I knew you, and before you were born I consecrated you; I have appointed you a prophet to the nations" (Jeremiah 1:5). Paul said that God had set him apart, even from his mother's womb (Galatians 1:15). God did not violate the free moral choice of Jeremiah or Paul, but He had His mind on them before they were born. God can devise, plan, and even predestine, without interfering with the free choice of His creation. We

may not *understand it*, but we can *stand on it* because of
the clear teaching of God's Word.

If you want to know how important the church is to
God, consider His choosing the church to be His elect
people before the foundation of the world. God made
this choice before He created anything. We often convey our priorities regarding a given circumstance to
someone by saying, "When that happened, I first
thought of. . . ." It is our way of revealing what we
considered at that moment to be most important to us.
By the probing instrument of God's Word, we can see
in a similar way what is most important to God by
looking at what was first in His mind: "He chose us in
Him before the foundation of the world." The church
as His chosen ones, as His elect people, was in God's
mind before the creation of the world.

How dear the elect are to God! They have been in
the mind of God from before the beginning of time.
This truth should enliven and strengthen us with divine encouragement.

CHOSEN FOR HOLINESS

Third, Paul said that we have been chosen for
holiness. He wrote, ". . . He chose us in Him before the
foundation of the world, *that we should be holy and
blameless before Him*" (Ephesians 1:4; emphasis mine).
We have been chosen for a purpose.

God has chosen the church to be His people and to
reflect His character or likeness. He has ordained that
His church be holy. Peter said, "But like the Holy One
who called you, be holy yourselves also in all your
behavior; because it is written, 'You shall be holy, for
I am holy'" (1 Peter 1:15, 16). Holiness means being
cleansed of sin and being set apart for God's sacred use.

God has also chosen His people to be blameless. This word means "without blemish" or "without fault." It indicates the goal of the people of God. We are to strive to live faultless lives before Him. Although we will never completely achieve this ambition in this life, it is the continual attitude of our hearts. Our strivings after holiness and blamelessness will not be realized until we stand before His throne in eternity. Christians, because of the cherished directives of their Lord, seek to live before God so that no legitimate accusation can be brought against them.

God planned or predestined our salvation in Christ before the foundation of the world, but we must choose to come into the sphere of salvation, the body of Christ, to be saved.

Paul also said that God "predestined us to adoption as sons through Jesus Christ to Himself" (1:5). He has chosen us to be His children. Adoption in this context means "to receive all the rights, privileges, and responsibilities of sonship." At the moment of adoption, we receive all that sonship in God's family implies. God predestined—determined beforehand, decided in beginningless eternity past—that He would adopt those who came into Jesus and would make them His children, giving them all the rights, riches, and responsibilities of His divine family.

Suppose you were called by a radio station and were told, "You have been chosen. We have selected you." You would immediately ask, "Chosen for what?"

Suppose the caller said, "We have chosen you, but we don't know what for. We didn't have anything special in mind when we picked you out. All we can tell you right now is that you are the chosen one. We had thousands of names in a basket, and when the drawing took place, you were chosen. So we have called to congratulate you." The excitement of being the chosen one would immediately fade when you heard, "We don't know what you were chosen for." You would no longer feel chosen or exceptional. The thrill of being chosen would be lost in the confusion of its meaning.

God has a purpose behind His choosing. God chose us to receive His salvation in Christ, to be adopted as His sons, and to live holy and blameless lives as His very own people in this world. He has chosen us to live set apart as His called out people with a divine mission.

Holiness and blamelessness are maintained by a consistent commitment to God's Word. We have been set apart or called to holiness through obedience to God's will, and our living in His will makes us faultless or blameless before Him. Let us take to heart the words of our brother Peter:

> Therefore, brethren, be all the more diligent to make certain about His calling and choosing you; for as long as you practice these things, you will never stumble; for in this way the entrance into the eternal kingdom of our Lord and Savior Jesus Christ will be abundantly supplied to you (2 Peter 1:10, 11).

CHOSEN BY GRACE

Fourth, we are chosen by grace. Paul said that God chose us *"according to the kind intention of His will,* to the praise of the glory of His grace, which He freely bestowed on us in the Beloved" (Ephesians 1:5, 6; emphasis mine). In other words, this choosing was initiated and consummated by the goodness and kindness of God.

What is the "kind intention of His will"? God's will has commandments, directions, and precepts. His entire will, in all of its scope and subjects, has a basic intention, an ultimate motivation, and a gracious design. What is this basic intention? Is it not salvation from sin and life with Him? In other words, He seeks the best for us. All that God has done, He has done out of His benevolent interest in our true well-being. Peter said, "The Lord . . . is patient toward you, not wishing for any to perish but for all to come to repentance" (2 Peter 3:9). Paul wrote, "This is good and acceptable in the sight of God our Savior, who desires all men to be saved and to come to the knowledge of the truth" (1 Timothy 2:3, 4).

The existence of the church, as the chosen people of God, is "to the praise of the glory of His grace, which He freely bestowed on us in the Beloved" (Ephesians 1:6). God planned the church, prophesied the coming of the church, sent Jesus to lay the foundation of the church, sent Jesus to die on the cross to purchase the church, miraculously started the church on Pentecost, and has providentially guided the preaching of the gospel—but all of this was done as a fulfillment of His compassionate intent for the salvation of the world. The result of His divine action, the existence of the church, is to the praise of the glory of His grace. The church cannot boast of starting from nothing and becoming a worldwide body. It can only glory in God's gracious intent and actions. Our glory is His grace.

Have you ever known anyone who constantly sought your best interest? Have you known one whose attitude, instead of being "me first," has always been "you first"? Has anyone preferred you in everything? If you could take the image of the most unselfish and generous person you have ever known and multiply that image a million times, you would have only a beginning of a picture of what God is like. Everything He does is in accordance with His loving kindness.

With gratitude for His grace, we should rejoice in the salvation we have in Christ, the mission He has given us, and the glorious future we have with Him as the chosen of God in endless eternity future. The heart of every saint should be constantly singing the theme song of the matchless grace of God. The superabundant grace of God should produce in us gratitude, praise, faith, and obedience.

CONCLUSION

Truly, the Holy Spirit through the pen of Paul has taught us that the church is the elect of God. He has told us that God chose us in Him, chose us from eternity, chose us for holiness, and chose us by His grace. We are the apple of His eye. We were His first thought as He planned the creation of the world, and we are His main thought now.

Anyone who is outside of Christ, outside the sphere of the chosen, should choose to enter His body without delay. When I was in high school, exceptional students were chosen to be placed among the "Who's Who" of the high school yearbook. Only a few were chosen, and the choices were based upon the students' popularity, superb talents, and excellent records. God's "Who's Who" is the church. Being among His "Who's Who" is a choice we make, not one that God makes. He places us among this elect group through our faith and obedience to Christ, not because of our popularity, talents, or records. Through His loving grace bestowed upon us in His Beloved, Jesus Christ, God invites all the non-elect to enter Christ's body and become one of the elect, one chosen for salvation, abundant life, and eternal life in heaven.

Elect to be among the elect. Choose to be one of the chosen ones. Decide to be one of God's predestined children.

QUESTIONS FOR STUDY AND DISCUSSION

1. Would you say that all the members of Christ's body are chosen of God?
2. What spiritual blessings are found in Christ according to Paul in Ephesians 1:4-6?
3. What is the difference between the predestination of a group and the predestination of a person?
4. What does the word "predestination" mean?
5. What is the difference in meaning of "foreknowledge" and "predestination"?
6. How can we know that we have been chosen of God?
7. When did God choose us in Him?
8. What has God chosen us to do or to be?
9. Define the word "holiness."
10. What does the phrase "chosen by grace" mean?
11. How does the phrase "chosen of God" encourage you?
12. How do we become one of God's chosen ones?

For Preaching and Teaching Purposes: Sermon or Teaching Type: Basic pattern; deductive; expository. Subject: The church. Theme: The church, the elect of God. Title: The Elect of God. Preaching or Teaching Portion: Ephesians 1:4-6. Proposition: (Declarative) The church is the chosen of God. Interrogative Question or Probing Question: How? Key Word: Ways. Major Points: I. Chosen in Him; II. Chosen From Eternity; III. Chosen for Holiness; IV. Chosen by Grace. Sermonic or Teaching Objective: To persuade the non-Christian to enter the Lord's church.

6

The Family of God

"So then you are no longer strangers and aliens, but you are fellow citizens, with the saints, and are of God's household" (Ephesians 2:19).

If you were handed a blank sheet of paper and asked to list the ten most satisfying blessings God has given the human race, what would you list? Which ten do you consider to be God's richest and most helpful benefits to mankind?

Most people, I believe, would put the family at the top of that list. Countless joys and supportive relationships have been experienced through the family from the beginning of its creation in the Garden of Eden to the most recent marriage ceremony. The majority of people would probably say that most of their happy memories cluster around the homes in which they grew up and/or the homes in which they currently live. Furthermore, I believe that all but a few people would say that they receive their greatest strength and assistance in living from their family members. Truly, the family was given to the human race by a loving heavenly Father who designed the home to give warm, sympathetic encouragement to our spirits.

In light of how meaningful the family is to us, we should not be surprised that it is used as a figure in the Scriptures to help us visualize the nature of the New Testament church. The use of the words "family" and "household" in the Scriptures compels us to see the church as the family of God. When we become Christians, we are born into God's spiritual family, the church (John 3:5; Ephesians 2:19). To say it another way, when we obey the gospel of Christ and enter the body of Christ, God adopts us as His children (Ephesians 1:5). Paul pointed to this adoption as the end result, the chief reason for Christ's coming into the world: "But when the fulness of the time came, God sent forth His Son, born of a woman, born under the Law, in order that He might redeem those who were under the Law, that we might receive the adoption as sons" (Galatians 4:4, 5).

NEEDS

All human beings possess certain standard needs that are met only by the physical family. What are these needs? First, each of us needs *a sense of belonging*, or "roots." The physical family provides a social stability. It gives us a niche in this world which belongs to us and to us alone.

Second, we need *a sense of security*, the assurance that we are a part of a community which will care for us should we ever become mentally, socially, or physically helpless. The physical family supplies this security for us. It gives us a shelter from life's storms. It provided for us when we were babies and were unable to care for ourselves. It provides for us when we become sick or broken in spirit, and it will provide for us when we become old and feeble, living in our second childhood. It is our refuge, our haven, our rock of support.

Third, we need *a sense of identity*. We have an inner urge to know who and what we are. To some extent, our physical families answer this yearning.

In the church of the New Testament, a Christian experiences a sense of spiritual belonging.

Fourth, we need *a sense of acceptance,* the security of knowing that we can be ourselves, free from make-up and masks. The physical family loves us for what we are—not for what we are going to be or for what we have been. In our physical families we do not have to achieve to be accepted. If we are unable to be the best or do the best, we are still loved and still have a place among our relatives. We do not have to earn the love we receive; it is given without strings or demands.

Human beings also have spiritual needs which correspond somewhat to the emotional, social, and physical needs which are satisfied by the physical family. Some people recognize these spiritual needs in themselves, while others do not. Whether we recognize them or not, they are real and must be met for us to live in this world in true happiness. The human personality and spirit have a spiritual dimension. When these characteristics are ignored or neglected, even though we may enjoy a type of social and physical happiness, we cannot enjoy the spiritual happiness and fulfillment which God intended for us.

What if I sought to clean out a closet simply by removing the spider webs? Would I not find myself frequently removing other spider webs? A spider makes webs, and as long as the spider remained in my closet, he would continue to build webs there.

What if I found water running all over the bathroom floor? How successful would I be in removing the water if I simply mopped it up? The water would be coming from some source, and until that source could be found and eliminated, I would continually be mopping up water from the bathroom floor.

The spiritual needs that are common to every human being do not go away. They are not quenched by our pretending that they do not exist. For us to experience normal physical happiness and spiritual joy, these physical and spiritual needs must be met.

NEEDS MET

The spiritual needs we all possess are satisfied by another family unit, the family of God. In His spiritual family, God is the Father (1 John 3:1), Christians are brothers and sisters (1 John 5:1), and Jesus is the elder brother (Romans 8:17). Paul referred to this heavenly family as "the church." He told Timothy, "I am writing these things to you, hoping to come to you before long; but in case I am delayed, I write so that you may know how one ought to conduct himself in the *household of God*, which is *the church of the living God*, the pillar and support of the truth" (1 Timothy 3:14, 15; emphasis mine).

In the church of the New Testament, a Christian experiences *a sense of spiritual belonging*. He has a heavenly Father to pray to, walk with, and live for. He has an elder brother to pray through, learn from, and lean on. He lives as part of a community of believers who love each other as brothers and sisters and work together for God's glory—not as an organization but as a spiritual family.

In God's family, we have *a sense of spiritual security.* We know that our heavenly Father loves us and will provide for us. He even provides for our physical needs. As He taught His followers not to worry, Jesus urged us to remember that our Father knows our needs and will take care of us: "Do not be anxious then, saying 'What shall we eat?' or 'What shall we drink?' or 'With what shall we clothe ourselves?' For all these things the Gentiles eagerly seek; for your heavenly Father knows that you need all these things" (Matthew 6:31, 32). Likewise, our Father provides for our spiritual needs. Jude reminded us of this heavenly care in the doxology with which he closed his letter by referring to God as one "who is able to keep you from stumbling, and to make you stand in the presence of His glory blameless with great joy" (Jude 24).

Our need for *a sense of spiritual identity* is also met in God's family, the church. Before conversion, we wandered without purpose or direction, but through being born into the family of God, we became God's own possession. Peter wrote of this change:

> But you are a chosen race, a royal priesthood, a holy nation, a people for God's own possession, that you may proclaim the excellencies of Him who has called you out of darkness into His marvelous light; for you once were not a people, but now you are the people of God; you had not received mercy, but now you have received mercy (1 Peter 2:9, 10).

Paul even referred to God's family as God's inheritance (Ephesians 1:18). As members of God's family, Christians have an eternal inheritance—heaven; God has an inheritance too—Christians!

God's family likewise provides us with *a sense of spiritual acceptance*. As we come to God in obedient faith and live before Him in trust and sincere obedience, we are accepted as His children. He bestows His special love upon us and puts in our hearts His Spirit, which cries, "Abba! Father!" (Galatians 4:6). In Christ, we can say with Paul, "There is therefore now no condemnation for those who are in Christ Jesus" (Romans 8:1). This does not mean that repentance and growth are no longer expected; it means that He receives us where we are and tenderly guides us to become what we ought to be. Someone has said, "He loves us as we are, but He loves us too much to leave us as we are."

I remember trying to lead a young married woman to Christ in London, England, several years ago. She was a beautiful young mother with one child. After a few months of marriage, her husband had left her, and she was trying to rear her child by herself. Apparently, her home life was not much when she was a child either. In our conversation, I said to her, "Through Christ, you can be saved and have a beautiful home!" My remark did not encourage her at all. I wondered why, and then I realized that this young woman had no idea of what a beautiful home was. She had never seen the home as attractive and wonderful. Her experiences had created in her mind an image of the home which was anything but supportive, strengthening, and loving; it was hard for her to visualize the home as beautiful. However, anyone who has seen a home which meets the normal physical, emotional, and spiritual needs of its members knows how beautiful the home can be when properly structured and led by Christ.

Like this young woman, many people cannot visualize how the church meets our spiritual needs. They have not been around a true New Testament church. They have not seen the church as the spiritual family of God. Therefore, it is hard for them to envision what they are missing as they live apart from the church of Christ. It is the duty of Christians to keep reminding people in this condition of what the church is and how the true church as the family of God answers to the spiritual dimensions of our lives.

Only through God's family can we find the peace, security, purpose, and identity that our innermost beings long for. True happiness cannot be ours outside of this family, the church.

NEEDS BEAUTIFULLY MET

To visualize the church as God's family, let us reflect on Luke's sketch of the Jerusalem church. His depiction shows the beautiful characteristics of God's family in the daily lives of the early Christians:

> And they were continually devoting themselves to the apostles' teaching and to fellowship, to the breaking of bread and to prayer.
> ... And all those who had believed were together, and had all things in common; and they began selling their property and possessions, and were sharing them with all, as anyone might have need. And day by day continuing with one mind in the temple, and breaking bread from house to house, they were taking

their meals together with gladness and sincerity of
heart, praising God, and having favor with all the
people. And the Lord was adding to their number day
by day those who were being saved (Acts 2:42-47).

Each Christian had a sense of belonging, for "all those
who had believed were together and had all things in
common" (Acts 2:44). Each member had identity, for
no one was valued above another, and the whole
congregation responded to the needs of any suffering
member. Everyone enjoyed acceptance. Day by day
people were added to the Lord's body and were received with joy by the congregation. Each member
enjoyed a security which could only be provided by a
community type of life. They sold their "property and
possessions, and were sharing them with all, as anyone might have need."

This congregation of God's family engaged in regu-
lar worship with prayer, praise, teaching, fellowship,
and the observing of the Lord's Supper (Acts 2:42).
They adored their heavenly Father, recognized the gift
of grace which came through their elder brother, Jesus
Christ, and lived in gladness and sincerity of heart.
They enjoyed the security of the community life of the
church, the benevolent care for this life, and the assurance of eternal life through Jesus in the world to come.

While I was preaching for a week for a small congregation several years ago, I noticed a little trailer
house that had been moved next to the church building. I assumed it was a makeshift extra classroom
which they had placed there. I asked a member, "What
is your little trailer house for?" "That is for our widow,"
the member explained with a smile. He further said,
"A Christian man of this congregation died recently,

leaving his wife all alone. She has had difficulty making ends meet and making the decisions she has had to make. So we moved this little trailer house in near the church building. We're letting her live in it so that she will have the security and the assistance she needs. She didn't want to live here without being of service in some way, so we let her do the janitorial work that is needed for the building." I thought as I listened to this explanation by the member, "This is the beautiful care and concern that should characterize God's family."

CONCLUSION

Do you not want to be a member of God's family? Do you realize that your life cannot be complete until you have entered God's family, the church? Outside of His family, you will be missing the spiritual stability, security, acceptance, and identity that only membership in His family can give.

Every child shudders at the thought of being an orphan, and every adult's heart cries out with pain when he sees an orphan. No one wants to be an orphan, and no one wants to see an orphan. We cannot altogether prevent the abandoning of children by the cruel circumstances of life or by human injustice; all we can do is reach out to orphans in love, sympathy, and assistance. No one, however, needs to be a spiritual orphan. Through the gospel, anyone can come into the family of God, be adopted as a child of His, and receive the love and sonship that all other children receive.

We enter God's family by a spiritual birth. Jesus said, "Truly, truly, I say to you, unless one is born of water and the Spirit, he cannot enter into the kingdom of God" (John 3:5). We are led by the Spirit through the Word of God to believe in Christ (John 8:24), to repent of sin (Acts 17:30), to confess Jesus as Christ and Lord (Romans 10:10), and to be baptized into Christ (1 Corinthians 12:13). Peter said, "For you have been born again not of seed which is perishable but imperishable, that is, through the living and abiding word of God" (1 Peter 1:23).

God receives as His children those who are born of the water and the Spirit. He gives them His Spirit (Galatians 4:6), the blessings of His family (Ephesians 1:3), and an eternal inheritance (Ephesians 1:11). The children of God, consequently, live with a sense of belonging, security, acceptance, and identity.

Are you a child of God?

QUESTIONS FOR STUDY
AND DISCUSSION

1. List the joys that you have experienced through the home.
2. How does one enter the family of God?
3. When does God adopt us as His children?
4. List the standard needs that each person has, and describe how the family meets these needs.
5. Compare our spiritual needs with the standard human needs.
6. Describe the spiritual family of which a Christian is a part.
7. How does the family of God give us spiritual security?
8. How does the family of God give us a sense of spiritual belonging?
9. How does the family of God give us a spiritual identity?

10. How does the family of God give us a sense of spiritual acceptance?
11. Use the Jerusalem church as an illustration of how being in the church meets our spiritual needs.
12. Can one be complete until he has entered God's spiritual family?
13. Is one who is outside the family of God somewhat like an orphan?
14. List the blessings you have especially enjoyed in God's spiritual family.

For Preaching and Teaching Purposes: Sermon or Teaching Type: Motivated sequence; inductive; topical. Subject: The church. Theme: The church, the family of God. Title: The Family of God. Preaching or Teaching Portion: None. Proposition: (Persuasive) You ought to be a part of the family of God. Interrogative Question or Probing Question: None. Key Word: None. Major Points: I. Needs; II. Needs Met; III. Needs Beautifully Met. Sermonic or Teaching Objective: To persuade listeners to become a part of the family of God.

7

God's Building

"In whom the whole building, being fitted together is growing into a holy temple in the Lord; in whom you also are being built together into a dwelling of God in the Spirit" (Ephesians 2:21, 22).

The greatest building enterprise in the Old Testament era must have been Solomon's construction of the temple of the Lord. The intention of building a "house for the Lord" was expressed first by David, but God told David through Nathan that the privilege would be given to Solomon because David had been a man of war (2 Samuel 7:5; 1 Chronicles 28:3). Nevertheless, David was permitted to gather materials for the temple's construction before his death.

Under Solomon's leadership, the temple was built of the finest and most expensive materials, with the greatest care and craftsmanship. Though built of stone, it was paneled with cedar and overlaid with gold. It was twice the size of the tabernacle (1 Kings 5:1—9:9; 2 Chronicles 2—7) and took seven and one-half years to complete. Located on Mount Moriah, perhaps it was built near the place where Abraham came to offer Isaac.

Ten thousand[1] Israelites were conscripted to work on the temple (1 Kings 5:13, 14) and 150,000 non-Israelites were used as laborers on it (1 Kings 5:15; 2 Chronicles 8:7-10). The non-Israelites were persons taken in war, sold in debt, or homeborn servants. They were divided into two groups—seventy thousand burden bearers and eighty thousand quarry men. The supervisors of all these laborers numbered 3,850.[2] In other words, a total of 163,850 men worked continuously to construct the temple. This tremendous number of laborers and supervisors indicates how immense this building project was.

Solomon's prayer at the dedication of the temple (2 Chronicles 6:3-42) is one of the most beautiful prayers in the Scriptures. At the close of his prayer, he offered 22,000 oxen and 120,000 sheep in sacrifice to the Lord (1 Kings 8:62, 63; 2 Chronicles 7:4, 5). The chronicler said, "Now when Solomon had finished praying, fire came down from heaven and consumed the burnt offering and the sacrifices; and the glory of the Lord filled the house. And the priests could not enter into

---

[1]Thirty thousand were conscripted to serve, but only ten thousand were used each month. Thus, each of those conscripted served one month out of every three (1 Kings 5:13).

[2]Second Chronicles 2:18 gives the number 3,600 for the Canaanite officers. Second Chronicles 8:10 gives the number 250 for the Israelite officers. This would give a total of 3,850 supervisory officers. First Kings 5:16 gives 3,300 as the number of the subordinate officers, while 1 Kings 9:23 gives 550 as the number of the superior officers. This would give a total of 3,850 supervisory officers as well. Thus, 2 Chronicles and 1 Kings harmonize on the number of supervisory officers, but they do look at the supervisors from different viewpoints.

the house of the Lord, because the glory of the Lord filled the Lord's house" (2 Chronicles 7:1, 2).

The temple stood as the magnificent house of the Lord for the nation of Israel until Nebuchadnezzar destroyed it in 586 B.C.

One could easily think that this temple of the Old Testament was the greatest building ever built for God, but this is not the case. A far greater building was built for God by Jesus. It is called by the New Testament writers "the church," and it is the most unique and glorious structure ever built for God in the history of the world.

In Ephesians 2 Paul gave one of the sharpest contrasts in all of the New Testament between being outside of Christ and being a Christian. He described the difference in the form of a "before-and-after" picture. For instance, before one becomes a Christian, Paul said, he is dead. He is walking according to the course of this world, under the power of the devil, living like the sons of disobedience (Ephesians 2:1-3). After one becomes a Christian, Paul said, he is forgiven. He is in Christ, and he is saved by grace (Ephesians 2:4-10). As Paul concluded this contrast, he referred to the oneness we have in Christ, whether we are Gentiles or Jews. In doing so, He used three figures to refer to the church: a city (2:19), a family (2:19), and a building (2:20, 21). His description of the church as God's building is one of the most beautiful descriptions of the church given to us by the Holy Spirit.

So then you are no longer strangers and aliens, but you are fellow citizens with the saints, and are of God's household, having been built upon the foundation of the apostles and prophets, Christ Jesus Him-

self being the corner stone, in whom the whole building, being fitted together is growing into a holy
temple in the Lord; in whom you also are being built
together into a dwelling of God in the Spirit (Ephesians 2:19-22).

In picturesque, figurative language, the Holy Spirit
called the church God's building. Looking at the church
through this imagery, we are reminded of its distinctive nature.

A "HUMAN" BUILDING

Unlike the temple of the Old Testament, the church,
God's New Testament building, is made out of people.
Each Christian provides the material out of which this
building is composed.

Paul said that the Gentiles who had become Christians were no longer strangers and aliens, but were
fellow citizens with the saints and were of God's
household, a family that had been built upon the
foundation of the apostles and prophets, with Jesus
Himself being the cornerstone. He said that Christians,
whether Jews or Gentiles, were fitted together into a
building of God. Peter made a similar analogy in
1 Peter 2:5: "You also, as living stones, are being built
up as a spiritual house for a holy priesthood, . . ."

The church is a building, but it is a spiritual building made out of people who have become Christians.
Each Christian is a spiritual stone in the building. All
Christians, as living stones, are joined or cemented
together by God's Spirit into an invisible, dynamic,
spiritual organism, which is figuratively likened to a
building.

Paul's picture is not that of hundreds of little organizations being grouped together to make up one giant building. The New Testament does not describe the universal church as being made up of all the denominations of the world. It rather describes each congregation of Christ's church as complete in and of itself, as a local manifestation of the universal church.[3] The universal church is made up of individual Christians from all over the world, each serving as living stones in this spiritual structure, the church.

We must never confuse the church with a physical building or the place of worship. The New Testament does not contain a single specific line about church buildings. Christians are commanded to assemble together regularly for worship (Hebrews 10:25), and this command would imply a place for assembling; but the place could obviously be, among other things, a house, an open place, or a particular building designed for that purpose. No detailed instructions are given in the New Testament about the place of worship. This is left up to the judgment and discretion of the Christians in each locality. They may choose to build a building in which they can regularly meet for worship, or they may choose to meet in a house or in an open place. We must remember that the church, God's building, is the Christians in a location, and not the place where they worship.

According to Paul, Christians are to see themselves as God's house, and each Christian is to see himself as an important part of that house. As a Christian walks down the street, an onlooker can say of him, "There goes a living stone in God's building, the church."

---

[3]F. F. Bruce, *The Epistle to the Ephesians* (Old Tappan, N.J.: Fleming H. Revell Co., 1961), 58.

The world will judge God's church by Christians, not by the building or place where Christians worship. Let us make sure that we live as God's building, that we live in harmony with our position in Christ's church.

A "LIVING" BUILDING

The fact that the church is a "human" building makes it evident that the church is also a "living" building. Solomon's temple of the Old Testament was made of inanimate materials, such as cedar, gold, silver, and ivory, but God's building today is made of living stones.

Paul never referred to the church as an institution. He implied, for instance, in the passage before us that the church is an organism, a spiritual building made of Christians, that is living and growing—a vibrant entity, not simply a group of people drawn together by common interests.

The building of which Paul wrote has no top. It has walls and a foundation, but no roof. Christians form the walls, and the foundation consists of the apostles and prophets, with Jesus as the cornerstone. Christ, as the cornerstone, bonds all the structure together. As people are converted to the Lord, they are added to the walls of this building; and since this is true, the building continually grows higher and higher every time new Christians are born. The word translated "growing" in Ephesians 2:21 is used only one other time in the New Testament, in Ephesians 4:16, to refer to the bonding together of each part of the body into a living union which results in growth to the overall body.

Luke wrote of the church in Acts 2: "So then, those who had received his word were baptized; and there were added that day about three thousand souls" (v. 41). Two chapters later he said, "But many of those who had heard the message believed; and the number of the men came to be about five thousand" (Acts 4:4). In a short period of time, God's building grew from having in it three thousand living stones to having five thousand. Through the intervening years since that time, God's building has continued to grow. It is bigger now than it was this time last year. It will continue to grow until Jesus returns.

---

*The church is a building,
but it is a spiritual building
made out of people who
have become Christians.*

Peter referred to Christians as "living stones" (1 Peter 2:5), and Paul called them "living sacrifices" (Romans 12:1). Assuredly, everything about this building of God is living. God the Father, in the Scriptures, is called the "living God" (1 Thessalonians 1:9). The Bible is "living and active" (Hebrews 4:12). Jesus, according to Peter, is the "living stone" (1 Peter 2:4). The hope which Christians have is real and authentic; and consequently, it is a "living hope" (1 Peter 1:3). The way into which Christians have entered through their obedience to Christ is "a new and living way" (Hebrews 10:20). Jesus, as the eternal Christ, our mediator, "always lives" to make intercession for us in heaven (Hebrews 7:25). We have been promised that even death cannot take away our life in Christ, for if we believe in Him, though we die yet shall we live (John 11:26).

A Christian is not a part of an organization. He is a living stone in a living, growing, spiritual house. We are making daily contributions to the growth and beauty of God's building. We have been joined together with other Christians to make a house that never stops growing. When we lead a soul to Christ, we add another living brick to the house of God. Conversely, if we were to destroy another Christian in some way, we would remove a living stone from God's house. Every Christian is joined to all other Christians; we live with each other and for each other, that jointly we might provide a building for God.

A "SPIRIT-INDWELT" BUILDING

Houses are made to live in, and God's building is no exception. His spiritual house is indwelt by His Spirit.

Paul said, ". . . the whole building, being fitted together is growing into a holy temple in the Lord; in whom you also are being built together into a dwelling of God in the Spirit" (Ephesians 2:21, 22). Paul also told the Corinthians, "Do you not know that you are a temple of God, and that the Spirit of God dwells in you?" (1 Corinthians 3:16).

God has a dwelling place upon earth even as He does in heaven. His dwelling place on earth is the church. He meets with and dwells among His family through the Spirit. The church is the visible part of God on earth; God daily lives in and works through His building, the church.

I grew up on a farm six and one-half miles from Springdale, Arkansas, in the Sonora community. Just across from our house, beyond a stream and a field, stood an old house which was empty most of the time while I was growing up. The house had been occupied by an aged couple, one of whom was confined to a wheelchair. I do not remember much about the couple, for I was only a small boy when they lived in the old house. When the couple died, the old house was left empty for some reason until it was torn down many years later. I can remember going into that old house after it had been vacant for a long time. The house had remained as the couple had left it—with furniture, dishes, beds, and other things still in place. It gave me an eerie feeling to walk through it. Having been empty for some time, it smelled of dust, mold, and deterioration. Newspapers and magazines were lying throughout the house as mute voices of the life and activities of the couple who had lived there years before. The obvious reason I had such a spooky feeling as I looked around in the old house was that the house was uninhabited. It was a shell, a furnished house with no life in it. Houses which have been vacant for a while and have been without the laughter and love of life are a pitiful sight. They usually become blots upon the landscape.

If the church were uninhabited, like that old house, it would be as worthless as it was. However, the true church is not a traditional relic from the past that is empty of life and energy; it is inhabited by the Spirit of God! Jesus built it as a place for God to dwell in the world.

Paganism had its temples throughout the Roman Empire. In Ephesus stood the ornate temple of the Asiatic goddess Diana, or Artemis. Judaism had its temple in Jerusalem and its synagogues scattered throughout the Roman world, where its members fought to keep the law of Moses alive long after God had done away with it. The most beautiful and elaborate of the temples of the world, however, is God's temple. His temple is not made with hands, but by God Himself; it shines with a glory and grandeur unequaled by any of man's temples, for God Himself dwells in it. Upon the divine foundation of the apostles and prophets, and Jesus as the cornerstone, God lays each living stone, each newborn Christian, upon another. Each is put into a cherished place in the wall of the building by the gracious hand of God in such a way that all the living stones fit exactly together. He builds on it day by day as people in India, Africa, Austria, America, Ukraine, Russia, and all parts of the world are converted to Christ. Then, in this spiritual, invisible, growing temple, God dwells through His Spirit!

This truth should come to our hearts with a great challenge. We are the temple of God in the world! Let us live with wisdom and holiness, obedience and faith!

CONCLUSION

A great and glorious truth was declared by Paul in Ephesians 2:19-22: The church is God's building. As this building, it is "human," "living," and "Spirit-indwelt."

It is said that a building contractor was hired by a wealthy man to build a mansion for him while he traveled abroad. The contractor was given free use of a large sum of money for the expenses of the building project. He was placed totally in charge of the construction. During the time of building, the contractor substituted shoddy, inexpensive materials for strong, dependable materials and put the difference in the price of the two types of material in his pocket. He managed to hide his secret behind paneling and paint, brick and mortar, floors and walls. When the owner returned, the house had been completed and was ready for occupancy. From the outside, the house gave every appearance that it had been built according to the owner's plans, but unseen to the human eye were inadequate, inexpensive boards and beams, pipes and ducks, tiles and sheetrock. How amazed and disappointed the contractor must have been when the owner handed him the key and said, "You may have this house as your own!" The contractor, in cheating the owner, had actually cheated himself.

We have not been charged *to build* a house—we have been commissioned *to be* a house! We are to be not just any house, but the very house of God! If we fail to come into Christ, to be a part of God's building as living stones, we cheat ourselves of the greatest privilege God has given man. If we enter God's house but fail to live as God's house by substituting shoddy, inadequate living for the Christian life designed by God, once again we cheat ourselves, robbing ourselves of the unexcelled opportunity of representing God by living as His dwelling place.

We cannot build a building for God as Solomon did, since the church is built by the Spirit of God through the Word of God. We can, however, *be* God's building through our submission to the gospel and through the daily squaring of our "living stones," our lives, with Christ as the cornerstone!

Are you part of God's building?

QUESTIONS FOR STUDY AND DISCUSSION

1. Describe the temple built by Solomon.
2. Using Ephesians 2, discuss the contrast between

the non-Christian and the Christian.
3. Paul depicts the unity of the church as what three figures in Ephesians 2:20, 21?
4. Discuss how God's temple today is a "human" building.
5. To what does the expression "living stones" refer—to churches or individual Christians?
6. How much information is given in the New Testament concerning a physical church building?
7. Discuss the place of the church building in our worship and our service to God.
8. How is the church a "living" building?
9. Explain how the church has walls and a foundation but no roof.
10. List the ways in which the church can grow.
11. Explain the meaning of the phrase "indwelt by the Spirit."
12. Compare the church with a pagan temple, accenting the difference that God's Spirit makes.
13. Discuss the difference between being given the charge to *build* a house and the charge to *be* a house.

For Preaching and Teaching Purposes: Sermon or Teaching Type: Basic pattern; deductive; expository. Subject: The church. Theme: The church as God's building. Title: God's Building. Preaching or Teaching Portion: Ephesians 2:21, 22. Proposition: (Declarative) The church is a unique building. Interrogative Question or Probing Question: How? Key Word: Ways. Major Points: I. A "Human" Building; II. A "Living" Building; III. A "Spirit-Indwelt" Building. Sermonic Objective: (Motivational) To motivate Christians to live as God's unique building.

8

Spiritual Israel

"But you are a chosen race, a royal priesthood, a holy nation, a people for God's own possession, that you may proclaim the excellencies of Him who has called you out of darkness into His marvelous light; for you once were not a people, but now you are the people of God; you had not received mercy, but now you have received mercy" (1 Peter 2:9, 10).

Not long ago, in one of my New Testament survey classes at Harding University, I spoke of Christ's coming into this world in "the fulness of time." Immediately a student's hand went up, and a young man asked with eager interest, "What does 'the fulness of time' mean?" I turned to Galatians 4:4, 5 and read Paul's words about Christ's birth: "But when the fulness of the time came, God sent forth His Son, born of a woman, born under the Law, in order that He might redeem those who were under the Law, that we might receive the adoption as sons."

I explained that "the fulness of time" was the time

that God in His eternal wisdom and forethought had appointed as the ideal time for Christ to come into the world as our Savior. To say it differently, divine planning and preparation preceded the Savior's birth. His coming was not a brief thought that flashed into our heavenly Father's mind and was rashly and impulsively acted upon; rather, His coming was intricately blueprinted in the mind of God before the foundations of the world were laid. When the necessary events took place, when the world was ripe for this divine intervention, Jesus was born. Appropriately, Paul called that juncture in history "the fulness of time."

The entire Old Testament period—the Patriarchal and Mosaical dispensations of time—formed a prelude for the coming of the Messiah. In the Patriarchal period, God chose Abraham and Jacob to be His servants through whom He would create a nation that He would call His own. He elected to call this nation "Israel," the name which He had given to Jacob. In the Mosaical Age, God brought His chosen nation under His law, which He revealed through Moses at Mount Sinai. He taught them to worship Him and to live as His holy people. Yet, all of God's actions during the Old Testament period were really the groundwork, the prearrangement, for bringing the Messiah into the world at "the fulness of time." Someone has said, "The story of the Old Testament is the story of a nation, and the story of the New Testament is the story of a Person."

Since the story of the Old Testament is the story of the nation of Israel, and since the creation of this nation was God's advance work for the bringing of the Messiah into the world, we should not be surprised that Paul referred to the Lord's church as the Israel of God:

"And those who will walk by this rule, peace and mercy be upon them, and upon the Israel of God" (Galatians 6:16). Nor are we surprised that Paul figuratively depicted the church with terms taken from God's covenant relationship with ancient Israel: "For we are the true circumcision, who worship in the Spirit of God and glory in Christ Jesus and put no confidence in the flesh" (Philippians 3:3). This depiction of the church as "Israel" should be highly significant to us, for it tells us that Christians are spiritual Israel today and have been set apart as God's own possession even as was ancient Israel!

Perhaps the most concise affirmation in the New Testament that the church is New Testament Israel is 1 Peter 2:9, 10. As Peter explained what it means to be a Christian in 1 Peter 1:22—2:10, he referred to the Christian's conversion (1:22-25), conduct (2:2, 3), and calling (2:4-10). He concluded by asking his readers to rejoice in the truth that Christians are God's chosen people, His true Israel.

Focus on Peter's reference to Christians as the Israel of God in 1 Peter 2:9, 10. This comparison confirms our special relationship with God and our special calling from God; it gives us reason to rejoice in the spiritual blessings that are offered to us in Christ. These verses will teach us that we are spiritual Israel.

A CHOSEN RACE

In describing the church as spiritual Israel, Peter first said that Christians are "a chosen race" (1 Peter 2:9). They have been elected, picked out, and set apart. They are God's divinely selected race of people, called out from all the peoples of the earth.

God had told Israel through Moses at Mount Sinai,

"For you are a holy people to the Lord your God; the Lord your God has chosen you to be a people for His own possession out of all the peoples who are on the face of the earth" (Deuteronomy 7:6). Again, He said of Israel, "Now then, if you will indeed obey My voice and keep My covenant, then you shall be My own possession among all the peoples, for all the earth is Mine" (Exodus 19:5).

However, in this last age of human history, Christians, not fleshly Israelites, are God's chosen race. The old Israel led to, formed the foundation of, and found fulfillment in the new Israel, the church. Paul said it was God's predetermined choice that all who enter Christ would be His chosen race of people:

> Just as He chose us in Him before the foundation of the world, that we should be holy and blameless before Him. In love He predestined us to adoption as sons through Jesus Christ to Himself, according to the kind intention of His will, . . . Also we have obtained an inheritance, having been predestined according to His purpose who works all things after the counsel of His will (Ephesians 1:4, 5, 11).

We have all had the disappointing experience of being left out, skipped over, or ignored. We have watched as others have been nominated or selected while we were completely passed by or left until last. Some of us went through this frustration as children when teams were chosen for a game; either others were chosen ahead of us, or we were by-passed entirely and left to keep score with grace. Some of us have lived through this type of ordeal as a list was read, with the honored ones being named first. We listened expectantly, only to hear our names read last and mispronounced. Episodes like these depress us and stay with us for a long time as haunting memories, crushing our self-image and convincing us that we are "nobody." These unpleasant circumstances treat us as poorly as the psychiatrist did the unfortunate man who came to him pleading, "Doc, I have an inferiority complex, and I don't know what to do about it." After the psychiatrist spent several sessions analyzing the patient, he told him, "Man, you don't have an inferiority complex; you're just inferior!"

That we are God's Israel today
is a mighty truth—one so powerful
that it supercharges us with
hope and assurance. . . .

Situations in which people are passed over usually develop because too much emphasis is placed on the abilities people have, how people look, how smart people are, or what people own. Consequently, when this happens to us, it is devastating, for it says to us that we are not talented enough, good looking enough, smart enough, or that we do not possess enough.

Christians, according to Peter, are God's chosen race. This is true, he said, not because we are the most talented, the best looking, or the smartest, or because we have the most, but because we are loved by God, have responded in faith and obedience to God's will, and have become His children, His church. Our status with God has resulted from God's mercy, not from our money or from human merit. Peter said, ". . . you had not received mercy, but now you have received mercy"

(1 Peter 2:10). Paul told Titus, "He saved us, not on the basis of deeds which we have done in righteousness, but according to His mercy, by the washing of regeneration and renewing by the Holy Spirit" (Titus 3:5). In our baptism into Christ, we received the mercy of God and became part of His chosen race.

That we are God's Israel today is a mighty truth—one so powerful that it supercharges us with hope and assurance which harassing circumstances and an unfriendly world cannot take from us. For example, it should infuse us with confidence and boldness in prayer to God. We can approach His throne with confidence at any time of need or whenever we wish to praise and thank Him. It should inspire us to live in God's strength, for being God's chosen people implies that God's storehouse of spiritual blessings is never closed to us (Ephesians 2:18).

Let us rejoice that we are His chosen race!

A ROYAL PRIESTHOOD

Second, Peter said that the church is "a royal priesthood" (1 Peter 2:9). Christians are God's priests today. As one body, they compose a kingdom of priests.

In Old Testament times, God provided His nation with access to Him through Levitical priests. He chose for the priests to come from the family of Amram from the tribe of Levi. They offered the sacrifices of the people to Him, and they led Israel in worship to Him in all the prescribed ways listed by the law of Moses.

God told the tribe of Levi, ". . . I am your portion and your inheritance. . . ." (Numbers 18:20). The Levites were given the honor of serving God uniquely in worship, in service, and in life. They were given access to God and an intimate relationship with Him.

Peter said in 1 Peter 2:9 that the Levitical priesthood is no longer in effect, and a new priesthood has been chosen by the Lord. Through the redemptive work of Christ, He has appointed His church as His Christian Age priesthood.

Not only has God called His church a priesthood; He has called it a "royal" priesthood. The church is a kingdom of priests or kingly priests. John wrote from Patmos to persecuted Christians, "And He has made us to be a kingdom, priests to His God and Father; . . ." (Revelation 1:6). Peter also said, "You also, as living stones, are being built up as a spiritual house for a holy priesthood, to offer up spiritual sacrifices acceptable to God through Jesus Christ" (1 Peter 2:5). The Christian can go directly to God through the assistance of the Holy Spirit (Romans 8:27) and through the intercessory work of Jesus, our Mediator and great High Priest (1 Timothy 2:5; Hebrews 7:26, 27). A Christian does not go to God through any intermediary other than Jesus Christ. He can stand before God as God's priest and make his appeal to God through Jesus Christ without the aid of ordained human priests, departed saints, or angels.

The word "priest" in Latin means "bridge-builder." The idea of a bridge illustrates the role of a priest during the Old Testament period. The priest was a kind of spiritual bridge between God and man. He brought God's will to man, and he offered man's requests to God. God went to the people through the priest, and the people went to God through the priest. How different it is today in the Christian Age! When one becomes a Christian, he becomes, at the moment of his entrance into Christ, a priest of God.

Our position as priests of God should compel us to

be consecrated to God's work and to utilize this sacred position He has given us to live in His fellowship. As the priesthood of God, we have a place of high privilege before God.

Let us rejoice that we are "a royal priesthood"!

A HOLY NATION

Third, Peter said that Christ's church is "a holy nation" (1 Peter 2:9). Figuratively speaking, the church is God's nation of people, a kingdom of people exclusively consecrated to Him.

Israel, as God's chosen nation, was called to holiness. Through Moses, God told Israel, "You shall be holy, for I the Lord your God am holy" (Leviticus 19:2). He further told them, "And you shall be to Me a kingdom of priests and a holy nation" (Exodus 19:6). With this call of Israel to holiness in mind, and even quoting perhaps from Leviticus 19:2, Peter told the readers of his letter, "But like the Holy One who called you, be holy yourselves also in all your behavior; because it is written, 'You shall be holy, for I am holy'" (1 Peter 1:15, 16).

Christians, God's nation of people, are to be like God. He is holy, and we are to be holy, imitating Him as dear children and reproducing in our personalities and actions our Father's likeness (Ephesians 5:1, 2).

The word "holy" simply means "set aside for sacred use." As applied to Christians, this word means that God's people have been set apart for undivided devotion and service to Him.

A Christian has citizenship in two nations—one in which he *dwells* and in another one to which he is *devoted*. He lives in this world as a citizen of the earth, but his governing citizenship is in the nation of God, a spiritual, heavenly kingdom. Paul wrote, "For our citizenship is in heaven, from which also we eagerly wait for a Savior, the Lord Jesus Christ" (Philippians 3:20).

As a Christian thinks of how he is a citizen of God's holy nation, he is at once comforted and challenged— comforted by His relationship to God and challenged by the heavenly calling that this relationship implies. Our conduct on earth, Peter said, should reflect at all times our citizenship in heaven. Holiness is to extend to every aspect of the Christian's life. Peter said, "... be holy yourselves also in all your behavior" (1 Peter 1:15). What we do, think, and say should reflect who we are.

One mother would always say to her children as she sent them to school or to some other activity which would separate them from her for a while, "Now remember who you are." She was hopeful that her reminder of who they were would motivate them to live up to that image, that their behavior would be in harmony with their belief. If Christians will remember who they are, God's holy nation, they will be constrained to live holy lives.

Let us rejoice that we are "a holy nation."

A PECULIAR PEOPLE

Fourth, Peter said that Christians are "a peculiar people" (1 Peter 2:9, KJV). The NASB has "a people for God's own possession," which more clearly translates the Greek phrase. The point is that Christians are God's private property, His own possession; and, in this sense, they are peculiar.

God said to fleshly Israel through Moses, "For you are a holy people to the Lord your God; the Lord your

God has chosen you to be a people for His own possession out of all the peoples who are on the face of the
earth" (Deuteronomy 7:6). He likewise said to them,

> And the Lord has today declared you to be His
> people, a treasured possession, as He promised you,
> and that you should keep all His commandments;
> and that He shall set you high above all nations which
> He has made, for praise, fame, and honor; and that
> you shall be a consecrated people to the Lord your
> God, as He has spoken (Deuteronomy 26:18, 19).

This beautiful concept of being a people which belongs
to God is applied by Peter to Christ's church, as he said
that now, in the Christian dispensation, the church is
the people of God's own possession. Paul made a
similar application of this phrase in Titus 2:14, when he
said that Christ "gave Himself for us, that He might
redeem us from every lawless deed and purify for
Himself a people for His own possession, zealous for
good deeds."

A few years ago, my family was with me in Washington, D.C., for a gospel meeting. During that week,
the brethren took us to some of the many historic sites
in that famous city. One of my most vivid memories is
that of visiting the theater where the beloved President
Abraham Lincoln was assassinated. Because of the
significance of the man, I was deeply impressed by the
site. The museum below that site reminded me that
insignificant, worthless items take on tremendous value
when they are owned or used by a renowned person.
A shoe which has little actual value is kept in a glass
case and is of inestimable worth because it was worn
by Lincoln on the day he was killed. Something trivial

became a priceless treasure because of who owned it. We Christians may not be worth much when taken by ourselves, but when we are seen as the people of God's own possession, a people owned and used by God, we really go up in price! It should do much for our self-worth, our sense of value, to realize that God has made us, out of all the people of the earth, His own possession.

Picture a young boy walking with his mother into a toy shop to buy a toy. As he scans the toys for sale, his eyes focus upon a broken sailboat which has pasted on it, "To Be Sold As Is." The sailboat is worth little "as is," but it becomes his choice. He pays the paltry price for it. As soon as he gets home, he goes to work on it. After putting a little glue here, a new piece of wood there, and a new coat of paint all over it, he can say to his boat, "I have bought you. I have repaired you. Now you are truly mine!" In a similar way, Christians belong to God. He has bought us with His Son's blood, He has remade us in our conversion to Him, and He is continually changing us as we walk with Him. Now He can say in redemptive splendor, "These are truly My own people." Every person who is converted to Christ is elevated to the high and wonderful status of being a person of God's own possession.

Let us rejoice that we are "a peculiar people."

CONCLUSION

The church, therefore, is spiritual Israel, the Israel of God today. We are a chosen people just as Israel of old was chosen. We have a priesthood today even as Israel did in Old Testament times. As Israel was God's holy nation, the church is God's holy nation today. Even as God called Israel to be a people of His own possession in the days of old, today, in the Christian dispensation, God regards Christ's church as His chosen possession.

On the fourth Thursday of each November, Americans celebrate Thanksgiving Day. While we understand that the New Testament nowhere commands that one particular day be a day of thanksgiving, it does picture thanksgiving as a daily spirit, a continual attitude. Thanksgiving in the New Testament is not an appointed day; it is a disposition. Paul characterized Christians as "always giving thanks for all things in the name of our Lord Jesus Christ to God, even the Father" (Ephesians 5:20). When we consider the blessings that Christians have, we can easily see why the New Testament says that every day should be a thanksgiving day. As "a chosen people," "a holy nation," "a royal priesthood," and "a people of God's own possession," we are blessed indeed and should make our way through each day singing, "Count your many blessings, name them one by one."

If you are not a Christian, you are missing out on the highest and greatest blessings which God offers to man. Now that you have seen the privileges God has bestowed upon His church, will you allow God to make you part of it?

QUESTIONS FOR STUDY AND DISCUSSION

1. Give a brief explanation of the phrase "the fulness of time."
2. How did the Old Testament period of time prepare the world for the coming of Christ?

3. How can Christians be referred to as God's chosen race?
4. Our status with God is based upon God's mercy and upon our faith and obedience. Compare this with a status which is based upon merit.
5. What part did the priesthood play in the Old Testament law?
6. Who were the priests in Old Testament times?
7. What does the word "royal" convey in connection with "priesthood"?
8. In what sense is the church a "holy nation"?
9. Describe how a Christian is a citizen of two nations.
10. Define the expression "a peculiar people."
11. What blessings come to your mind when you think of Christians as being God's special people?
12. How do we enter spiritual Israel today?

For Preaching and Teaching Purposes: Sermon or Teaching Type: Basic pattern; deductive; textual. Subject: The church. Theme: The church as New Testament Israel. Title: Spiritual Israel. Preaching or Teaching Portion: 1 Peter 2:9, 10. Proposition: (Declarative; didactic) The church is spiritual Israel of the New Testament. Interrogative Question or Probing Question: How? Key Word: Ways. Major Points: I. A Chosen Race; II. A Royal Priesthood; III. A Holy Nation; IV. A Peculiar People. Sermonic Objective: (Edificational) To motivate Christians to rejoice in their relationship to God in the church.

9

God's Temple

"Do you not know that you are a temple of God, and that the Spirit of God dwells in you?" (1 Corinthians 3:16).

Augustine, looking from man's emptiness without God, wrote, "Our hearts are restless, O God, until they find rest in Thee." It is reasonable to believe that God, looking from His longing for fellowship with man, says, "My heart yearns for you, O man, until you find rest in Me. I love you, and I delight in your salvation and fellowship."

Can we actually believe that the Almighty God wishes to have fellowship with man? Why would Jehovah God create this universe, the heavens and the earth, and man if this were not His desire? Who could believe that the all-knowing and all-wise God who created all things would make man as a toy, as a plaything, for His amusement as was believed of the capricious, childlike gods of mythology? The make-up of the world and the spiritual potential of man join in arguing that the God of the heavens and the earth seeks and finds joy in communion with us.

What we conclude through reason is the very affirmation of the Scriptures. God has said to His people, "I will dwell in them and walk among them; and I will be their God, and they shall be My people" (2 Corinthians 6:16). He has said of those whom He would redeem and bring into His fellowship, "I will be a father to you, and you shall be sons and daughters to Me" (2 Corinthians 6:18).

This truth of God's dwelling among His people must be seen in concert with the church. Under the new covenant, the church is the temple of God, a spiritual house (1 Peter 2:5), with each Christian as a living stone in that house (1 Peter 2:5), and the whole building forming the dwelling of God in the Spirit (Ephesians 2:21, 22).

Recognizing the church as the temple of God reveals another facet of the nature of the church. The word "temple," which is rich with Old Testament connotations, brings us into a deeper realization of the church's relationship to God and of its walk with God.

Therefore, for a better understanding of the church of Christ, let us ask, "How is the church the temple of God?"

A MEETING PLACE

First, the church is the temple of God in the sense that the church is the meeting place of God and man. The church is where God and man unite in fellowship.

When Israel arrived at Mount Sinai, God gave them His law and a place of worship through Moses. The place of worship was called "the tent of meeting," because it was the place where Jehovah met with

Moses, His priests, and His people (Exodus 29:42). Continual burnt offerings were offered at the doorway of the tabernacle, because God had said, ". . . I will meet with you, to speak to you there. And I will meet there with the sons of Israel, and it shall be consecrated by My glory" (Exodus 29:42, 43). God had designed a place where He and His people could meet in fellowship.

Now, under the last will and testament of Christ, the new covenant, God has chosen the church as His meeting place with His people. When we obey the gospel of Christ, we are washed from our sins in the blood of Jesus and are brought through adoption into God's family (Ephesians 1:5; Galatians 4:6). Those who have become Christians have not only come to know God, but have come to be known of God and have come into God's inheritance (Ephesians 1:14; Galatians 4:9). We have become sons of God, and as sons, we have become heirs of eternal life through Christ (Romans 8:17; Galatians 4:7). We have entered the church, the family of God, wherein we walk with God in friendship and fellowship, in communion and camaraderie.

Years ago the church was blessed by the preaching of Marshal Keeble. He had a picturesque way of illustrating spiritual truths, a way which held the attention of his audience and riveted truths to the mind. As he was preaching one night on baptism, he quoted 1 Peter 3:21: "And corresponding to that, baptism now saves you—not the removal of dirt from the flesh, but an appeal to God for a good conscience—through the resurrection of Jesus Christ." Brother Keeble then said, "Three are present at baptism. First, the one being baptized, the sinner, is present to be baptized. Second, the preacher, the one baptizing the sinner, is present to do the baptizing. Third, God is present. When the preacher baptizes the sinner, God and the sinner meet in the water."

Marshal Keeble's illustration brings out a telling point. God has commanded baptism as part of His plan for salvation. It is the final command which we obey as we come to Christ. As believing, penitent sinners are baptized into Christ, they are united with God and Christ (Romans 6:3; Galatians 4:6), meeting them in a saving relationship in the water.

The wonderful news of the gospel is that God has provided a place where He meets with man in sacred fellowship, and that place is the church. In essence, God has said to man in this Christian dispensation in His Word, "I will meet with you in My temple, Christ's body, the church. I have provided for you a way of salvation so that you may meet with Me for spiritual life and holy fellowship."

A DWELLING PLACE

Second, the church is God's temple because it is God's dwelling place. God not only meets with us in His temple, but He also dwells with us in it. Through the church, God lives among His people.

Regarding the tabernacle under the law of Moses, God said to Israel, "And I will dwell among the sons of Israel and will be their God. And they shall know that I am the Lord their God who brought them out of the land of Egypt, that I might dwell among them; I am the Lord their God" (Exodus 29:45, 46). The tabernacle and all that pertained to it reminded Israel of God's presence among them. In harmony with the promise God had made to Israel, He filled the tabernacle with His glory (Exodus 40:34). As a manifestation of the presence of God, a cloudy pillar stood above the Most Holy Place of the tabernacle by day and a fiery pillar stood over it at night. When Israel moved by day, the cloudy pillar went before them as an expression of the guidance of God, while the fiery pillar provided God's guidance by night (Exodus 40:36-38; Numbers 9:15-23). Through the tabernacle, God dwelt among His people, leading them and living among them.

In the New Testament, the church is the dwelling place of God through His Spirit. Paul wrote to the church at Corinth, "Or what agreement has the temple of God with idols? For we are the temple of the living God; just as God said, 'I will dwell in them and walk among them; and I will be their God, and they shall be My people'" (2 Corinthians 6:16). Paul said of the Gentiles who had become Christians in Ephesians 2,

> So then you are no longer strangers and aliens, but you are fellow citizens with the saints, and are of God's household, having been built upon the foundation of the apostles and prophets, Christ Jesus Himself being the corner stone, in whom the whole building, being fitted together is growing into a holy temple in the Lord; in whom you also are being built together into a dwelling of God in the Spirit (Ephesians 2:19-22).

God dwells in Christians in two ways: First, His Spirit dwells in each individual Christian, using the Christian's heart as His temple. Paul used the idea of the Spirit's indwelling as an argument for Christians to keep their bodies clean from immorality: "Flee immorality. . . . Or do you not know that your body is a temple of the Holy Spirit who is in you, whom you have from God, and that you are not your own?" (1 Corinthians 6:18, 19).

Second, God's Spirit indwells the corporate body of Christians, the church. Paul wrote regarding the church at Corinth, "Do you not know that you are a temple of God, and that the Spirit of God dwells in you?" (1 Corinthians 3:16). The Greek word Paul used for "you" in this verse is plural. The Spirit obviously had in mind the body of believers, the church, and not just the individual Christian.

As God's temple, the church is the meeting place of God, the dwelling place of God, and our place to worship God.

All of us have questions about how God indwells His people. However, one truth we can be sure about is that His indwelling is in accordance with His Word, for God works through His Word (Ephesians 6:17). Paul, in these passages, did not explain in detail God's indwelling; he just affirmed it. The truth Christians should find in these passages is that God is with us individually and corporately. He dwells among us; He lives in us.

At eighty years of age, Moses met God at the burning bush at Horeb (Exodus 3:1). God said to him, ". . . I will send you to Pharaoh, so that you may bring My people, the sons of Israel, out of Egypt" (Exodus 3:10). Moses did not believe that he was the one to go to Egypt for God, but after God answered his excuses, Moses left the burning bush and went on his way to Egypt, charged with the mission of delivering op-

pressed Israel. Moses soon saw the difference between *meeting with* God and *walking with* God. He had met with God at Horeb and received his commission. Leaving Horeb, he had walked away with God. Moses had been told by the Lord, "Certainly, I will be with you, . . ." (Exodus 3:12). God kept His promise and walked with Moses as he led Israel through all the plagues, through the Red Sea, and to Mount Sinai.

As the church, the temple of God, we have not only met God in Christ, but God continually dwells in us and walks with us. How reassured and confident Christians should be! As we faithfully live the Christian life, we walk in the daily fellowship of God. We do not face one trial or one difficulty without His blessed companionship and strength.

John wrote, "If we say that we have fellowship with Him and yet walk in the darkness, we lie and do not practice the truth; but if we walk in the light as He Himself is in the light, we have fellowship with one another, and the blood of Jesus His Son cleanses us from all sin" (1 John 1:6, 7).

A PLACE OF WORSHIP

Third, the church, as the temple of God, is a place of worship. The Christian is a walking cathedral.

Peter said, "You also, as living stones, are being built up as a spiritual house for a holy priesthood, to offer up spiritual sacrifices acceptable to God through Jesus Christ" (1 Peter 2:5). He also said, "But you are a chosen race, a royal priesthood, a holy nation, a people for God's own possession, that you may proclaim the excellencies of Him who has called you out of darkness into His marvelous light" (1 Peter 2:9). As God's priests today, Christians may offer up praises to God through

Jesus at any time and at any place. Because of Jesus, we are urged by the writer of Hebrews to confidently approach God: "Let us therefore draw near with confidence to the throne of grace, that we may receive mercy and may find grace to help in time of need" (Hebrews 4:16).

Jesus told the woman from Samaria at Jacob's well that worship would no longer be confined to a specific location, to a divinely appointed mountain or building. He said, "Woman, believe Me, an hour is coming when neither in this mountain, nor in Jerusalem, shall you worship the Father" (John 4:21). In the future, He was saying, worship would be acceptable because it was offered in spirit and in truth, not because it was offered at the right physical place. He further said to this Samaritan woman, "But an hour is coming, and now is, when the true worshipers shall worship the Father in spirit and truth; for such people the Father seeks to be His worshipers" (John 4:23). Jesus was speaking of the Christian dispensation, when Christians, as priests of God, would worship God through Him anywhere, anytime.

Having complete access to God, Christians are blessed with the privileges of worship (John 4:23), atonement provisions (1 John 2:1), and divine power (Ephesians 1:19). As priests of God who have been richly and superabundantly endowed, therefore, "let us continually offer up a sacrifice of praise to God, that is, the fruit of lips that give thanks to His name" (Hebrews 13:15).

CONCLUSION

The church is the temple of God! What a challenging truth! As God's temple, the church is the meeting

place of God, the dwelling place of God, and our place to worship God.

Are you a member of Christ's church? Think of all that you are missing if you are outside of Christ. Outside of Him, you are outside of His meeting place with man. You have not truly met with God or come to Him regardless of how religious you may be. Outside of Him, you cannot dwell with God. You cannot live and walk with Him where you are. Outside of Him, you cannot worship God acceptably. You cannot worship Him where you are in His appointed way and from His designated place, the Christian's heart. If you are outside of Christ's body, decide now to enter His body (Romans 6:3) so that you may walk with God in life and in eternity.

To enjoy God's presence and provisions, you must be in the place of God's purpose. It was God's purpose for Moses to go to Egypt and deliver God's people. What if Moses had gone in the opposite direction? He simply would have gone without God's presence, provisions, and power. This is true because he would have been outside of God's purposes. God told Jonah to go to Nineveh, but Jonah headed for Tarshish. The Bible says, ". . . So he went down to Joppa, found a ship which was going to Tarshish, paid the fare, and went down into it to go with them to Tarshish *from the presence of the Lord*" (Jonah 1:3; emphasis mine). Jonah could have gone to Nineveh with God's companionship, but not to the city of Tarshish. Nineveh was the place of God's purpose; Tarshish was not.

Anyone who comes into the church, God's temple, comes into the purposes of God and into that body to whom God has said, "I will be a father to you, and you shall be sons and daughters to Me" (2 Corinthians

6:18). When one becomes a Christian, his house of clay, his body, becomes the glorious temple of God!

QUESTIONS FOR STUDY
AND DISCUSSION

1. Augustine said, "Our hearts are restless, O God, until they find rest in Thee." What does this statement mean?
2. What evidence do we have that God wants us to have fellowship with Him? List the reasons for believing this to be true.
3. List the Scriptures which teach that God desires our fellowship.
4. How is the church the "meeting place" of God and man?
5. How did God and man have fellowship in the Old Testament period?
6. Discuss how the church is God's "dwelling place" in the Christian Age.
7. How did the tabernacle remind Israel of God's dwelling place?
8. Discuss the two ways in which God dwells in Christians (1 Corinthians 6:18, 19; 3:16).
9. How is the church of Christ a "place of worship"?
10. Discuss the physical location in connection with true worship.
11. Since the church is God's temple, list the blessings we enjoy today as opposed to the blessings which were enjoyed under the Old Testament law.
12. How do we enter God's temple today?

For Preaching and Teaching Purposes: Sermon or Teaching Type: Basic pattern; deductive; textual. Subject: The church. Theme: The church, the temple of God. Title: God's Temple. Preaching or Teaching Portion: 1 Corinthians 3:16. Proposition: (Declarative/didactic) The church is the temple of God. Interrogative Question: How? Key Word: Ways. Major Points: I. A Meeting Place; II. A Dwelling Place; III. A Place of Worship. Sermonic or Teaching Objective: To persuade the non-Christian to enter the Lord's church.

10

Christ's Flock

---

*"And I have other sheep, which are not of this fold;
I must bring them also, and they shall hear My voice;
and they shall become one flock with one shepherd"
(John 10:16).*

*"Be on guard for yourselves and for all the flock,
among which the Holy Spirit has made you overseers,
. . ." (Acts 20:28).*

When I am overwhelmed by responsibilities, I think of the children's story about the discouraged clock. A grandfather clock counted the number of times he would have to tick each year, and the number was staggering to him. As he thought about that amazingly large number, he became so discouraged that he decided to quit ticking. He concluded that he just could not tick that many times. A fellow clock recognized his discouragement and began talking to him. He helped him to see that he would have to tick only one day at a time, one hour at a time, one minute at a time, one tick at a time. His admonition cured the grandfather clock's depression. Thinking of the truth that he would have to tick only one tick at a time revived his spirit, gave him a new outlook on life, and inspired him to begin ticking again.

Our Lord admonished, "Therefore do not be anxious for tomorrow; for tomorrow will care for itself. Each day has enough trouble of its own" (Matthew 6:34). One remedy to discouragement is to remember that life is lived only one day at a time.

Are you fearful? Do you worry about the tremendous ability of the Evil One to overcome God's people? Are you anxious about what tomorrow will bring? Are you troubled about fulfilling your obligations to the Lord?

Jesus addressed these fears and many others with an illustration in John 10. He spoke of His followers as His flock and pictured His relationship to them as being analogous to a shepherd's relationship to his sheep. When you are fearful or anxious, remember His illustration. It will comfort you with the realization that "greater is He who is in you than he who is in the world" (1 John 4:4). It will also remind you of the great love and care Jesus' followers receive.

Jesus used this illustration[1] to speak of His relationship with His followers at that time, as He anticipated

---

[1]John called Jesus' analogy "a proverb." He used the word *paroimia*, which some versions of the New Testament have translated "parable"; but the New Testament Greek word for "parable" is *parabole*, an entirely different word. John never used the word *parabole* in his account of our Lord's life, and Matthew, Mark, and Luke never used the word *paroimia* in their accounts. In light of the word John used, Jesus' illustration or analogy should be seen as something like an extended proverb, the notion of a mysterious saying full of compressed thought, rather than that of a simple comparison.

the relationship He would have in the future with His followers whom He would call His church (Matthew 16:18). The analogy depicts the good shepherd laying down His life for the sheep (John 10:15, 17, 18). This is a direct reference to Jesus' crucifixion, the means by which He purchased the church (Acts 20:28; Ephesians 5:25). He spoke of other sheep that would come to Him: "And I have other sheep, which are not of this fold; I must bring them also, and they shall hear My voice; and they shall become one flock with one shepherd" (John 10:16). These verses show us that the church today should be seen as Christ's flock.

Thinking of the church as His flock will cause us to appreciate what Christ does for His church. Therefore, let us ask, "What is Christ's relationship to His flock, the church? What does Christ, as the shepherd, do for the church?"

CHRIST IS LORD OF THE CHURCH

The first truth that is evident from this analogy is that Christ is Lord of the church. The shepherd to which Jesus likens Himself owns the sheep; he is the sovereign ruler of the flock.

Whoever enters the flock becomes Christ's possession, even as a sheep would be the personal property of the shepherd. This concept of ownership goes in two directions: First, it implies that the sheep live for the shepherd. Since we belong to Christ, we are Christ's servants (Philippians 1:1). Second, it indicates that the shepherd lives for the sheep. As the owner of the sheep, the shepherd loves the sheep, is responsible for them, and provides for their upkeep. Ownership carries with it a heavy responsibility, and the good shepherd fulfills that responsibility.

Someone has said, "No one cares for children quite the way their parents do." The reason for this truth is clear: Parents recognize their children as peculiarly theirs. They brought their children into the world; they are of the same flesh and blood; they are responsible for them. They rejoice over their children, provide for them, and plan for their future.

We can be sure that Christ, the Almighty Son of God, will care thoroughly and tenderly for His own. David, in a psalm of thanksgiving, gave thanks for God's continual care for his physical needs: "I have been young, and now I am old; yet I have not seen the righteous forsaken, or his descendants begging bread" (Psalms 37:25). Jesus admonished His disciples in the Sermon on the Mount, "Do not be anxious then, saying, 'What shall we eat?' or 'What shall we drink?' or 'With what shall we clothe ourselves?'" (Matthew 6:31). Jesus said, "The thief comes only to steal, and kill, and destroy; I came that they might have life, and might have it abundantly" (John 10:10). Our good shepherd owns us and sees to our physical and spiritual needs.

This truth should affect us greatly. Christ's ownership of us means that He is in charge of us. Why should we worry? Why should we be afraid? Trust in the good shepherd who watches over you. Our only obligation is to follow Jesus as Lord; He handles everything else.

CHRIST LEADS THE CHURCH

Second, the "good shepherd" analogy reminds us that Christ leads the church. As sheep follow their shepherd, the church follows Christ. We recognize His voice and answer to it. Jesus said,

Truly, truly, I say to you, he who does not enter
by the door into the fold of the sheep, but climbs up
some other way, he is a thief and a robber. But he who
enters by the door is a shepherd of the sheep. To him
the doorkeeper opens, and the sheep hear his voice,
and he calls his own sheep by name, and leads them
out (John 10:1-3).

Each night, the shepherd would bring his sheep
into a community fold, a walled-in type of corral with
only one entrance. At that gate a porter was stationed
throughout the night. In the morning, the shepherd
would come and be recognized by the porter. He
would then be allowed to enter the fold, call his sheep
to himself, and lead them out to pasture. A thief or
robber would have to climb over the wall to enter the
fold. He would not be recognized by the porter and
would not be allowed to enter the fold.

Jesus further said, "When he puts forth all his own,
he goes before them, and the sheep follow him because
they know his voice. And a stranger they simply will
not follow, but will flee from him, because they do not
know the voice of strangers" (John 10:4, 5). In the
morning, as the shepherd would come to take his
sheep out of the fold, he would merely walk to the front
of the fold and call for them. His sheep would hear his
voice and run to him. When the sheep left the fold, they
had no protection but that of the shepherd. They were
totally dependent upon him to lead them out where
they could graze unafraid and be free from harm.

The shepherd was altogether the master of his
sheep. The sheep would go wherever he led them.
They were under his guidance and wisdom. Of all the
animals, sheep are characteristically followers. They

do not have a good sense of direction. On their own, they are accidents just looking for a place to happen. Properly led, however, they enjoy a good life.

We are like sheep in this respect. Without leadership, we stumble like blind men groping for a helping hand. Isaiah wrote, "All of us like sheep have gone astray, each of us has turned to his own way; . . ." (Isaiah 53:6). Jeremiah said, "I know, O Lord, that a man's way is not in himself; nor is it in a man who walks to direct his steps" (Jeremiah 10:23). We must have the proper guidance, or tragedy awaits us.

Jesus is to us what a good shepherd is to the sheep—He is our leader and guide.

Jesus is to us what a good shepherd is to the sheep—He is our leader and guide. He is the Head of the church (Ephesians 5:23), our Captain of Salvation who is bringing us to glory (Hebrews 2:10). We look to Him as "wisdom from God, and righteousness and sanctification, and redemption" (1 Corinthians 1:30). Being aware of our inabilities and of who He is causes us to realize that the central task of the Christian race is that of "fixing our eyes on Jesus, the author and perfecter of faith" (Hebrews 12:2). We do not just look *at* Him; we look *unto* Him as our Leader and Lord.

Imagine trying to drive an automobile with no headlights in the middle of the night over a mountainous road which has steep climbs and descents, sharp turns, and canyon-like shoulders. To do so would be suicide. An accident would be inevitable; you just would not know where or when the accident would happen. This situation is an accurate picture of a sinful person who is trying to make His way through this world without divine guidance. Like a person driving a car without headlights on a dangerous road, he is headed for ruin!

Jesus assures us, however, that He gives His sheep divine guidance and that the mountains, valleys, ditches, and canyons of life should hold no fear for us. With Jesus as our leader, we can relax in safety as we make our journey through life.

A group of hunters beginning their journey through a jungle region of Africa asked their guide, "Do you have a map?" He answered, "I am your map!" This is Jesus' relationship to us—through His Word, He is our map! Someone has said, "One can hear Jesus without following Him, but one cannot follow Jesus without hearing Him." We listen to His Word and follow Him.

Facing the realization that we have a poor sense of direction could be discouraging to us, but recognizing that we have an all-wise, unerring shepherd leading us turns our disappointment in ourselves into an unending appreciation for our relationship with Jesus. Our most crucial need is supplied by our almighty, all-wise Leader.

CHRIST LOVES THE CHURCH

Third, this analogy pictures Christ as the good shepherd who loves the church and willingly lays down His life for it. He cares for the sheep and will protect them with the sacrifice of His life. Jesus said,

> I am the good shepherd; the good shepherd lays down His life for the sheep. He who is a hireling, and

not a shepherd, who is not the owner of the sheep, beholds the wolf coming, and leaves the sheep, and flees, and the wolf snatches them, and scatters them. He flees because he is a hireling, and is not concerned about the sheep. I am the good shepherd; and I know My own, and My own know Me, even as the Father knows Me and I know the Father; and I lay down My life for the sheep (John 10:11-15).

Jesus, as a good shepherd, stands in stark contrast to two other types of shepherds. First, He is not like a hireling, a shepherd who only serves for what he can make from his service. A hireling is a mercenary; he is paid to do his duty. While he is not evil or wicked, he does not have the personal concern for the sheep that a true shepherd has. Once his duty is fulfilled, he has no further sense of obligation toward the sheep. Second, Jesus is not like the unfaithful shepherd who fails in his task because of selfish concerns. Ezekiel wrote of the unfaithful shepherd in vivid language as he spoke for God:

> Those who are sickly you have not strengthened, the diseased you have not healed, the broken you have not bound up, the scattered you have not brought back, nor have you sought for the lost; but with force and with severity you have dominated them. And they were scattered for lack of a shepherd, and they became food for every beast of the field and were scattered. My flock wandered through all the mountains and on every high hill, and My flock was scattered over all the surface of the earth; and there was no one to search or seek for them (Ezekiel 34:4-6).

Jesus is different from these shepherds. He is the

"good" shepherd. The term for "good" which Jesus used is more like "beautiful." He is the beautiful shepherd. He is not paid to serve, but He paid with His life to serve because He loves the sheep. He paid for their protection with His life's blood. When danger threatens—when a wolf or lion comes to hurt the flock—He does not hide to save Himself from harm. He puts the lives and the care of the sheep ahead of His own life.

Jesus has an intimate relationship with the sheep, similar to His relationship with the Father—close, loving, with oneness and commonality, according to John 10:14, 15. Jesus used the word "know" four times in these two verses to convey the relationship He has with His sheep. He stands with His sheep in darkness and light, in suffering and health, in danger and peace. He knows His sheep personally. Every sheep has His constant attention, love, and concern. He encourages, cares for, and tenderly watches over His sheep; He shields them with His strength in a time of danger.

The story is told of an older couple who were trapped in a flooding area after a dam had broken. The water was rising, and rescue operations were underway. The engulfing water made every trip to higher ground crucial. Every minute was precious. The older couple waited together on the roof of their house for help to come. When a rescue boat came, it had room for only one. The husband insisted that his wife take the seat, but she adamantly refused. She wanted to stay with her husband regardless of the risk. Time could not be wasted; the water was rapidly advancing. The man in charge of the rescue boat said to them, "I'll take these passengers to safety and hurry back for both of you. I hope I can make it, but we're taking a great risk. The water is rising too rapidly." He rushed to higher ground, unloaded his passengers, and returned, only to find that the house and the couple had been swept away by the surging, rushing water. This dear wife had stayed with her husband, knowing that they might have to die together. Is there any love greater than this? Yes. "Greater love has no one than this, that one lay down his life for his friends" (John 15:13). To die that others might live is the greatest love of all. Our shepherd has this type of love, the deepest type of love, a love that is stronger than death. He lays down His life for the sheep (Ephesians 5:25).

All evidence indicates that the Gospel of John was written toward the end of the first century, perhaps A.D. 85-95. The first readers, therefore, knew not only that Jesus had said He would lay down His life for the sheep, but that He had actually done it. He had manifested the ultimate expression of care for His sheep by dying for the church.

How bracing this truth should be to us! We have an Almighty Lord who leads us. He loves each of us and has pledged not only His guidance, but also His love and protection. Paul said, "For if while we were enemies, we were reconciled to God through the death of His Son, much more, having been reconciled, we shall be saved by His life" (Romans 5:10). If Jesus loved us enough to die for us when we were yet in our sins, how much more will He look out for our salvation now that we are trying to live for Him and be His sheep?

CONCLUSION

Christ's analogy in John 10 declares that the church is the flock of Christ and is made up of all the sheep that belong to Him. He said, "And I have other sheep, which are not of this fold; I must bring them also, and they shall hear My voice; and they shall become one flock with one shepherd" (John 10:16). The "other sheep" to whom He referred must be, or at least include, Gentiles who would hear His voice and come into His flock. His analogy has only one flock and one shepherd. Either we are in His flock, under the one shepherd, or we are not. Either we are in His church, the New Testament church, or we are not.

One of the practical implications of the flock/shepherd analogy is that it calms our fears and drives away our anxieties. We know who we are, for we are His sheep; we know what to do, for we are guided by His voice; our future is secure, for we are protected by His life and death. We have a sense of belonging since He is our Lord; we have true knowledge because the Lord of heaven is our leader; and we have heavenly care from the Almighty Christ who was willing to lay down His life for us! If we know who we are, have infallible guidance, and have the sacrificial protection of Christ, why should we be afraid? Faith in our shepherd dispels our fears.

We can appropriate the words of Psalm 23 and apply them to Jesus even though they were written by David about God during the Mosaical Age:

> [Jesus] is my shepherd,
> I shall not want.
> He makes me lie down in green pastures;
> He leads me beside quiet waters.
> He restores my soul;
> He guides me in the paths of righteousness
> For His name's sake.
>
> Even though I walk through the valley of the
> shadow of death,

I fear no evil; for Thou art with me;
Thy rod and Thy staff, they comfort me.
Thou dost prepare a table before me in the
    presence of my enemies;
Thou hast anointed my head with oil;
My cup overflows.
Surely goodness and lovingkindness will follow
    me all the days of my life,
And I will dwell [with my Savior, the good
    shepherd] forever.

Years ago as a very young preacher, I attended the funeral of a brother in Christ. The gospel preacher who spoke at the funeral was my physical brother. According to what I remember, the man who had died was only in his forties at the time of his death. In his remarks, my brother told of this Christian man's last words before he died. He said that he softly quoted Psalm 23, and as the final word of that psalm was whispered, his breathing stopped. In his last moments of life, he found comfort in quoting Psalm 23.

Peace and serenity enter troubled and fearful hearts when God is contemplated as our shepherd. This analogy which pictures Jesus as the good shepherd and His followers as His sheep can minister to our anxieties in a similar way.

If you are not in Christ's flock, remember that you must enter His flock through the only door—Christ Himself. Christ put a smaller analogy (John 10:7-9) in the midst of His detailed and larger one (John 10:1-5, 10-18). He said, "I am the door; if anyone enters through Me, he shall be saved, and shall go in and out, and find pasture" (John 10:9). Christ later said, "I am the way, and the truth, and the life; no one comes to the Father, but through Me" (John 14:6). The flock of Christ is

entered through Christ when one obeys His words
(John 8:24; Luke 13:3; Matthew 10:32, 33; Mark 16:16).

Come to Christ, the good shepherd. Enter His flock,
allow Him to be the shepherd of your life, and partake
of the abundant life which He gives (John 10:10). In His
flock, you will have salvation (John 10:9), abundant life
(John 10:10), freedom from fear (John 10:12), love (John
10:15), guidance (John 10:4, 5), and eternal life (John
10:17). Can you think of a better way to live than as a
sheep in the flock of Christ?

QUESTIONS FOR STUDY
AND DISCUSSION

1. What do you do when you become discouraged?
2. How many parables are given in the Gospel of
   John?
3. Describe what Christ's being Lord of the church
   means to us and to Him.
4. How does the fact that Christ cares for His flock
   encourage you?
5. Discuss the context and specific meaning of John
   10:10.
6. Describe the inability of sheep to guide themselves.
7. How does a shepherd provide leadership for his
   sheep?
8. What kind of future do people who refuse divine
   guidance have?
9. Describe a "hireling," and compare him with a
   good shepherd.
10. Give the characteristics of an unfaithful shepherd
    as pictured in Ezekiel 34:4-6.
11. Observe the use of the word "know" in John 10,

and comment upon the meaning of this word (note
verses 14 and 15).
12. Who are the "other sheep" of John 10:16?
13. How does an individual become one of Christ's
sheep?

For Preaching and Teaching Purposes: Sermon or Teaching Type:
Basic pattern; expository. Subject: The church. Theme: The church,
Christ's flock. Title: Christ's Flock. Preaching or Teaching Portion:
John 10. Proposition: (Declarative/didactic) The church is Christ's
flock. Interrogative Question or Probing Question: How? Key Word:
Ways. Major Points: I. Christ Is Lord of the Church; II. Christ Leads the
Church; III. Christ Loves the Church. Sermonic or Teaching Objective:
To persuade Christians to rejoice in Christ's care for the church.

11

Christ's Bride

". . . for I betrothed you to one husband, that to Christ I might present you as a pure virgin" (2 Corinthians 11:2).

Some of the women students at Harding University jokingly say, "Do you know why God made man first? He wanted to make a rough draft before He made His masterpiece!" All jesting aside, woman, according to God's design, is a beautiful creature—the most beautiful of God's entire creation.

A woman is never more beautiful than on her wedding day. What husband can forget the radiant beauty of his bride as she came to pledge her heart and life to him at their marriage ceremony? Her loveliness at that moment will stay imprinted in his mind until old age veils his memory or death claims him.

No other image of the church can possibly elicit from our minds such appeal and emotion as does the word "bride." It ranks as perhaps the most picturesque of all the New Testament images for the church.

The term is used only by John as a description of the church. He intermingled the earthly and heavenly states of the church in his use of the word (Revelation 21:2, 9; 22:17). Jesus, however, alluded to the church as a bride in Mark 2:19, as did Paul in 2 Corinthians 11:2. Other such allusions include Paul's comparison in Ephesians 5:22-33 and his analogy in Romans 7:1-4.

Thinking of the church as the bride of Christ brings us to another view of the nature and character of the church. For a complete understanding of what the church is intended to be, we must weigh all of the terms, images, and figures which the Holy Spirit used to describe it.

What does this imagery of a bride suggest when applied to the church?

UNQUESTIONED LOYALTY

First, the term "bride" conveys faithfulness. A bride has made a commitment; she has entered into a covenant that requires love, loyalty, and life.

Paul feared that the Corinthians were turning from the true Christ to a false Jesus and a false gospel. Consequently, he used the strongest possible language to urge the Corinthians to steadfastness and purity: "For I am jealous for you with a godly jealousy; for I betrothed you to one husband, that to Christ I might present you as a pure virgin" (2 Corinthians 11:2). It is unthinkable for a bride to betray her husband, so Paul used the betrothal relationship to illustrate the fidelity that a Christian is to have toward Christ.

What illustration would be more suggestive of allegiance than the husband-and-wife union? Most of us have heard of husbands and wives who chose to face death together rather than be separated from each other. The devotion of their hearts to each other mattered more than life itself.

The church's only imperative is faithfulness to Christ. His people do not have to succeed, prosper, or even live—they only have to be true to Christ (Revelation 2:10). We must prize our commitment to Him more than we value any other relationship (Luke 14:26), possession (Luke 14:33), or allegiance (Luke 14:27).

UNIQUE IDENTITY

Second, the idea of the church's being the bride of Christ implies identity. We are a group of people who have narrowed down our loves to one love, and with this singleness of mind we have made a covenant with Christ. Hence, we belong to Christ and Christ belongs to us, even as a husband and wife belong to each other. We look to Christ as our Head and wear His name, and He takes us as His body on earth and calls us His church.

Marriage means a new identity for both husband and wife, but this is especially true for the bride, for as she enters the lifelong contract of marriage, she receives a new name, the name of her husband. Similarly, when we enter the church and become part of the "churches of Christ" (Romans 16:16), we enter into a new identity which springs from our union with Christ.

God has so arranged marriage that a husband and wife become one: "For this cause a man shall leave his father and his mother, and shall cleave to his wife; and they shall become one flesh" (Genesis 2:24). Likewise, in conversion, we become one with Christ (Romans 6:3). This oneness is so profound that it is best illustrated by the oneness that a husband and wife experience in marriage: "So husbands ought also to love their own wives as their own bodies. . . . just as Christ also does the church, because we are members of His body" (Ephesians 5:28-30).

Of the major commitments that a person makes, other than becoming a Christian, marriage may be the foremost. The marriage relationship is so unusually significant that the one who enters it must become a different person. He was *one* before marriage, but in marriage he is *two;* before marriage he was *himself,* but in marriage he *belongs to another.* In a similar way, as we enter the church of the New Testament, we become the body of Christ. We are no longer what we were; we have become *Christians,* individuals who are identified by our oneness with Christ.

UNSURPASSED RELATIONSHIP

Third, a bride sustains a special, ongoing commitment to the bridegroom. No relationship on earth falls into the same category as that of a bride and her bridegroom.

Paul detailed the bond the church has to Christ in Ephesians 5:22-33 with an extended parallel to the husband-and-wife relationship. His illustration explains the roles God has given to the husband and the wife in the Christian marriage, but his primary focus is the linkage which exists between Christ and the church (Ephesians 5:32).

In his comparison, Paul by inspiration placed the emphasis upon submission. As the bride of Christ, the church submits to Christ as her Head. He said, "Wives, be subject to your own husbands, as to the Lord. For the husband is the head of the wife, as Christ also is the head of the church, He Himself being the Savior of the body" (Ephesians 5:22, 23). The church looks to Christ as her leader even as a wife submits to her husband.

Someone has said, "The perfect government is a dictatorship if the dictator is perfect." The church submits to the perfect Christ and thus enjoys perfect leadership. The church looks to no man, to no group of men, to no headquarters on this earth for its authority. The true church of Christ has only one Head, Christ the Lord.

Whenever I discuss Ephesians 5:22-33 in a Bible class, I mention that verse 23 belongs to the wife, not to the husband, and verse 25 belongs to the husband, not to the wife. The word for the wife is "submission," and the word for the husband is "sacrifice." A good husband will have at least two qualities, according to Paul: (1) He will love his wife sacrificially even as Christ loved the church, and (2) he will seek to provide the highest quality of spiritual leadership for her. Likewise, according to Paul, a good wife will also have at least two qualities: (1) She will submit to her husband as her head, and (2) she will love him as the church should love Christ.

No one can have this exclusive bride/bridegroom relationship with Christ without entering and being His church. Just as no other woman can be given the same privileges as a man's wife, no other organization or institution—however renowned or committed to service—is given the privilege of a bride/bridegroom relationship with Christ.

UNLIMITED PROVISIONS

Fourth, being the bride of Christ means having the provisions of Christ's care and love. Who can totally comprehend the blessings that come to the bride of the King of kings and Lord of lords?

To begin with, Jesus provides *salvation* for His church. Paul referred to Christ as "the Savior of the body" (Ephesians 5:23). He brought this life to His church by laying down His life for her: ". . . just as Christ also loved the church and gave Himself up for her" (Ephesians 5:25). Further, Jesus *sustains* the church. Paul said that a husband is to nourish his wife "just as Christ also does the church" (Ephesians 5:29). Jesus guards the *sanctity* of the church and *secures* her future: "That he might sanctify her, having cleansed her by the washing of water with the word, that He might present to Himself the church in all her glory, having no spot or wrinkle or any such thing; but that she should be holy and blameless" (Ephesians 5:26, 27).

---

*Entrance into Christ's body brings
us under the care and provisions
of Christ even as the bride comes
under the loving care
of her husband.*

Children (and adults) enjoy the charming story of Cinderella. We are enchanted by the idea that a mistreated slave girl could eventually marry a prince. Let us take the story beyond its ending. What was "the rest of the story"? What was life like for Cinderella as the wife of the prince? How different life was for her! Formerly accustomed to poverty, slavish work, ridicule, and disappointment, she came to know luxury, riches, assistance, and a glorious future in her new home and life. Her marriage to the prince brought her a new identity, a new life, and innumerable pleasures.

Entrance into Christ's body brings us under the

care and provisions of Christ even as the bride comes under the loving care of her husband. Only the church has the promise of Christ's safekeeping.

UNPARALLELED PROMISE

Fifth, as Christ's bride, the church will enjoy the same future that Christ will enjoy. The church will go where Christ goes, receive what Christ receives, and live with Christ in eternity.

The specific use of the word "bride" in the New Testament in connection with the church is found in Revelation 21 and 22. John used the word to combine the nature of the church with its destiny. He first saw the "new Jerusalem, coming down out of heaven from God, made ready as a bride adorned for her husband" (Revelation 21:2). Later, John was told by an angel, "Come here, I shall show you the bride, the wife of the Lamb" (Revelation 21:9). He was then carried away in the Spirit to a great and high mountain and was shown "the holy city, Jerusalem, coming down out of heaven from God, having the glory of God. . . ." (Revelation 21:10, 11). Revelation closes with the invitation of the Spirit and the bride: "And the Spirit and the bride say, 'Come.' And let the one who hears say, 'Come.' And let the one who is thirsty come; let the one who wishes take the water of life without cost" (Revelation 22:17).

The church, according to the Spirit, is to be seen as the fiancée of Christ in its earthly state and as the wife of Christ in its heavenly state. This fits Paul's exhortation to faithfulness at 2 Corinthians 11:2: "For I am jealous for you with a godly jealousy; for I betrothed you to one husband, that to Christ I might present you as a pure virgin."

The fulfillment of the betrothal is the actual marriage. John described a vision of the new Jerusalem, the holy city, as it came down from heaven as a bride adorned for her husband; and he interpreted this vision as the church moving from betrothal into marriage. The figure is a blending of the nature of the church, which is symbolized by the term "bride," with the future of the church, which is portrayed in the heavenly city's coming down as the wife of the Lamb.

Jesus has promised to save His body, His church (Ephesians 5:23), and no other institution. The future of His church is pictured in Revelation in terms of the fulfillment of a previously-made promise and as a victory over the Evil One. Should you seek that eternal city, the Scriptures guide you to seek it through faithfulness to Christ in His church.

UNBLEMISHED BEAUTY

Sixth, the term "bride" suggests beauty. Nothing exceeds the loveliness of a bride. Her charm and grace are proverbial.

John wrote, "And I saw the holy city, new Jerusalem, coming down out of heaven from God, made ready as a bride *adorned for her husband*" (Revelation 21:2; emphasis mine). As Isaiah wrote of the blessings of the Lord, he used the attractiveness of a bride as an illustration: "I will rejoice greatly in the Lord, My soul will exult in my God; for He has clothed me with garments of salvation, He has wrapped me with a robe of righteousness, as a bridegroom decks himself with a garland, and as a bride adorns herself with her jewels" (Isaiah 61:10). He further compared God's faithful people to the radiance of a bride: "... and as the bridegroom rejoices over the bride, so your God will rejoice over you" (Isaiah 62:5).

A custom honored by many couples in America is not to let the bridegroom see the bride's wedding dress until she walks in for the marriage ceremony wearing it. Following this custom, the bride is truly "adorned for her husband." When the bridegroom first sees her, he finds her beauty to be inexpressible.

The church, Christ's bride, is clothed with garments of righteousness and the wedding dress of holiness. Paul wrote, "That He might present to Himself the church in all her glory, having no spot or wrinkle or any such thing; but that she should be holy and blameless" (Ephesians 5:27).

If the church is beautiful to Christ, it will also be beautiful to the world. It is like the cliché "Take care of your character, and your character will take care of your reputation." As the church remains pure through Christ's Word, and thus is beautiful to Christ, its reputation in the world will be as it should be.

By abiding in the Word, by being loyal to Christ, the church adorns herself for the marriage to Christ in heaven. We prepare ourselves for that special day by maintaining a spotless character and a blameless spirit before God.

CONCLUSION

What is more beautiful than a bride adorned for her husband? Beauty, purity, and enduring loyalty are all conveyed in the word "bride." It is easy to see why the Holy Spirit chose this image to express the church's nature. In this term, we see the unique relationship which the church sustains to Christ, the loyalty of the church to Christ, the provisions of Christ for the church, the identity Christ gives to the church, and the future

Christ has in store for the church. The figure brings to mind the advantages and aspirations we have as Christians, our obligations and our opportunities. It floods our minds with the lovely, glorious place of the church at the side of Christ.

Inasmuch as the church is the bride of Christ, who would not want to be a member of His church? What a privilege to be the bride of Christ! Whoever does not enter the body of Christ and live as a follower of Christ surely has not understood the nature of the church.

Suppose someone offered you a vast treasure and you could spend it as you chose. Would you accept it? Can you imagine anyone's refusing the *Reader's Digest* ten million dollar sweepstakes? If the money were awarded to you, would you be indifferent toward it? Would you say, "Ten million dollars, huh? Sorry, I'm just not interested"? The answer is obvious. You would exuberantly rejoice in the riches you had received.

Christ's invitation for you to enter His church and live as His bride transcends all earthly riches and positions of pleasure and glory. It invites you to enter into an eternal relationship with Jesus that will provide lavishly for you here and beyond our present ability to comprehend in eternity.

"And Peter said to them, 'Repent, and let each of you be baptized in the name of Jesus Christ for the forgiveness of your sins; and you shall receive the gift of the Holy Spirit.' ... And the Lord was adding to their number day by day those who were being saved" (Acts 2:38, 47).

QUESTIONS FOR STUDY AND DISCUSSION

1. List the characteristics of a bride.
2. Which New Testament writer specifically refers to the church as "the bride of Christ"?
3. What does it mean to be loyal to Christ?
4. How does marriage change our identity?
5. Would you say that marriage is one of the strongest commitments we make?
6. What does the word "submission" mean?
7. Discuss the statement "The perfect government is a dictatorship if the dictator is perfect." Relate this statement to Christ.
8. How is a husband to love his wife according to Ephesians 5:22-33?
9. What does Christ provide for His church?
10. What kind of future does Christ's church have? Describe this future in your own words.
11. What main characteristic comes to mind when you think of the church as the "bride of Christ"?
12. Has Christ promised salvation to His church? Has He promised salvation to any other church?

For Preaching and Teaching Purposes: Sermon or Teaching Type: Basic pattern; topical. Subject: The church. Theme: The church, the bride of Christ. Title: Christ's Bride. Preaching or Teaching Portion: None. Proposition: (Declarative/didactic) The word "bride" suggests aspects of the church's nature. Interrogative Question or Probing Question: What? Key Word: Characteristics. Major Points: I. Unquestioned Loyalty; II. Unique Identity; III. Unsurpassed Relationship; IV. Unlimited Provisions; V. Unparalleled Promise; VI. Unblemished Beauty. Sermonic or Teaching Objective: To persuade people to live as the bride of Christ.

12

God's Holy Priesthood

"... To Him who loves us, and released us from our sins by His blood, and He has made us to be a kingdom, priests to His God and Father; to Him be the glory and the dominion forever and ever. Amen" (Revelation 1:5, 6).

As a mature man and an American citizen, I have lived under two sets of laws. As a child, I lived under that group of laws which our country has for minors. At that time, I was not permitted to drive a car, own a house, have my own bank account, or vote. I had to live under the supervision of my parents. My signature on any document meant nothing unless it was cosigned by one of my parents. I was regarded as a child, and special laws governed my life and protected me.

Now, as an adult, I live under another series of laws. Within the limits of these laws, I can own and drive a car, own a house, have a personal bank account, and vote for public officials. Under this collection of laws, I am more of an individual, but with these personal privileges come personal responsibilities. I may choose to work and earn money, but I have the obligation of paying taxes on the money I have earned. I have the right to make decisions on my own without the authorization of my parents, but I will be judged by the law as responsible for my actions. It is a new set of laws under which I live as an adult, a set markedly different from the set under which I lived as a child.

The Jews of the first century found themselves in a similar circumstance. They experienced living under two sets of spiritual laws or covenants. They had been living under the law of Moses by sacrificing at the temple, observing annual festivals and feasts, going to God through specially appointed priests, and keeping all the other laws given to Israel through Moses. Then Christianity was inaugurated in Jerusalem on the first Day of Pentecost after the resurrection of Christ. As some Jews made the decision to follow Christ as His church, they entered into God's new covenant, leaving the law of Moses and coming under a new set of laws. As Christians under the new covenant, they would walk by faith, live according to the will of Christ as revealed through His apostles, and serve and worship God as Christ's spiritual body.

As the Jews made this transition from the law of Moses to Christianity, perhaps one truth that stood out in bold relief to them was that God no longer had a select group among His people who served Him as priests, but all of His people were His priests. According to the new covenant, Christ has taken all who have been washed in His blood and has made them "to be a kingdom, priests to His God and Father" (Revelation 1:6). In Christ, we are "a chosen race, a royal priesthood, a holy nation, a people for God's own possession" (1 Peter 2:9). We have been added to the church of Christ which is "being built up as a spiritual house for a holy priesthood, to offer up spiritual sacrifices acceptable to God through Jesus Christ" (1 Peter 2:5). This priesthood of all Christians should strike us as it must have struck the Jews, inspiring in us amazement, awe, and a deep sense of gratitude.

The priesthood feature of the church, when understood, will encourage every Christian. In the previous age, God honored the Levites by making them His priests; and in the present age, God has honored every person who has come into Christ by making him or her a priest in His kingdom.

Has this truth about the priesthood of all of God's children gripped us? Have we seen the significance of it? Let us give it more in-depth thought.

A PRIESTLY PRIVILEGE FROM GOD

Those who have become Christians have had a priestly privilege bestowed upon them. God has honored them with a special relationship with Him, just as He did His Old Testament priests.

The Mosaical priests were granted a distinctive fellowship with God. They lived daily in God's presence in a way not enjoyed by the other Israelites. At every camping site, their tents were located directly in front of the tabernacle, near the visible presence of God. When Israel settled in Canaan, the priests, along with the Levites, received God as their special possession, rather than an allotment of land. They did receive forty-eight cities and their surrounding pasturelands as places to live (Joshua 21:41), but they would be supported by the other tribes so that they could give their time totally to the service of God. Every sacrifice that would be brought by Israel to be offered at the tabernacle would be offered to God by a priest. God had set aside the priests to have a favored association with Him.

This intimate communion with God enjoyed only by the priests in Old Testament times is given in this Christian Age to every Christian. Anyone who comes to God through the gospel is adopted into His family and is looked upon as a person of "His own possession" (Titus 2:14). People who were once "not a people" are now the "people of God" (1 Peter 2:10). Those who were "far away" (Ephesians 2:17) from God have been "brought near" by the blood of Christ Jesus (Ephesians 2:13). God (John 14:23), Christ (Ephesians 3:17; Colossians 1:27), and the Holy Spirit (1 Corinthians 6:19, 20) dwell within us. We walk daily in the fellowship of the Father, Jesus Christ (1 John 1:3), and the Holy Spirit (Romans 8:5).

Moses came down from Mount Sinai with the first copy of the Ten Commandments engraved upon two tablets of stone only to find the Israelites falling down before a golden calf in idolatrous worship. He threw the tablets to the ground, as if to say, "Before I could get down from Mount Sinai with these ten commandments, you people had already broken them!" He ground the calf into powder, scattered the powder over the surface of the water, and made the people drink it. Moses took a position at the gate of the camp and said, "Whoever is on the Lord's side, come and stand beside me!" Immediately, the tribe of Levi fell in beside Moses in brave loyalty and support. Moses commanded the tribe of Levi to go throughout the camp and kill those who had been guilty of this idolatrous worship. They faithfully carried out his order, allowing themselves to be God's instruments of judgment. Because of their faithfulness to God, God honored them throughout the remaining Mosaical dispensation by bestowing upon them the privilege of being His chosen priests. Those of the family of Amram were His priests, and the rest of the Levites assisted them in the Lord's service. Thus, the Levites received the highest honor God can impart to anyone—that of being His chosen servants in the world!

Through Christ, anyone today may be granted the honor which God granted only to the Levites in Old Testament days. Whoever comes to Him in faith and obedience is added to God's set-apart people, His holy priesthood.

This amazing truth has a message for us. First, it should remind us that God has given His redeemed people significance and worth in His sight. We have been lifted from being nothing to being God's special possession. We are not just "a people"; we are "the people of God." In addition, this truth should clarify our mission in this world. We are servants of God in a particular sense. Further, this truth should produce in us an undying attitude of gratitude. We are where we are and what we are because of God's grace.

A PRIESTLY ACCESS TO GOD

Those who are members of the spiritual body of Christ have a priestly access to God. We do not have to go through any other human being in order to approach Him. Through Christ, we have an open approach to God.

The Jews could only reach up to God through a human priest. God spoke to the Jews through a prophet or priest, and the Jews sacrificed to God through the priest. The Jews had to have a human "go-between" to bridge the gap between them and God.

Now, in Christ, the Christian can go directly to God through Jesus. All barriers between God and man have been removed by the cross for both Jew and Gentile. At the end of a section on the unity that Jews and Gentiles have in Christ, Paul mentioned this access: "For through Him we both have our access in one Spirit to the Father" (Ephesians 2:18). Later, Paul wrote, "In whom we have boldness and confident access through faith in Him" (Ephesians 3:12). Jesus is the only mediator needed for the Christian to come to God: "For there is one God, and one mediator also between God and men, the man Christ Jesus" (1 Timothy 2:5).

I have two presidents in my life. The more immediate one is the president of Harding University, where I daily teach Bible. He is my boss. I see him every day in chapel, and I speak to him often in teachers' meetings and when I pass him in the hall. I visit with him at social functions and see him at worship services at the College church, where I worship when I am not away preaching. I speak to him so often and have been so closely associated with him for several years that I would call him my personal friend. I could telephone him at any hour of the day, and I would be allowed to speak to him about whatever I wished. If he could not come to the phone to talk with me, he would return the call as soon as he could.

The second president in my life is the President of the United States. I have never spoken to him personally. I have seen him in person only one time, and that was from some distance away as he rode in a car in a parade. All I really know about him is what I have read in the newspapers or have seen on T.V. I cannot say that I know him as a friend. I know nothing firsthand about his personal life, and he knows nothing about mine. If I should need to call him about an important matter, I would not be allowed to talk with him. I would only be promised that the message would be sent to him. He lives in a world far removed from mine. I have no real accessibility to his life and power except at the voting machine when our nation chooses its President every four years. What he does trickles down to affect me, but he never sees me, and I only see him from a distance.

Whoever comes to Him in faith and obedience is added to God's set-apart people, His holy priesthood.

What is the difference between these two presidents? It is simply this: I have access to one, and I do not have access to the other. The difference is in that one word: "access." My relationship with God, since I am a Christian, would be compared with my relationship with the president of Harding University. Through Christ, I have free and unhindered entrance to God. I can approach Him in prayer at any time. I walk daily in His companionship and strength. Because He is the Almighty God, He never needs to put me on hold or return a call when I pray. The door into His presence, because of Christ, always stands ajar for my entrance. He not only allows me to come into His presence, but He welcomes me into it. He seeks my fellowship, and I seek His. He is truly my heavenly Father.

The Jews under the law of Moses did not have the access to God that I have as a Christian. They went to

God through Levitical priests. God was their constant companion, but their access to Him was limited to an approach through a human priesthood.

This truth about priestly access which Christians enjoy should not only encourage us, but also should energize us. God welcomes us into His presence, enjoys our fellowship, and gives us freedom of approach to Him even as a father gives his children admittance to himself. Let us employ this opportunity of fellowship with God through prayer, companionship, and spiritual service.

A PRIESTLY FUNCTION FOR GOD

As Christians, we have a priestly function. We do the work of priests.

In Old Testament times, the priests offered the sacrifices to God for all of Israel. Only the priests could enter the Holy Place of the tabernacle as the worship of God was conducted. The common Israelite, as he stood at the entrance of the tabernacle, was represented in the tabernacle by priests. On the great Day of Atonement, the high priest would enter the Most Holy Place, into the presence of God, with the blood of the atoning sacrifice, through which the nation's sins would be cleansed until the next Day of Atonement. Beyond these worship responsibilities, the priests had a specific commission from God to teach His laws throughout Israel so that His nation would be confident of His will for them.

These holy functions of the priests during the Old Testament period find their parallel in what Christians are asked to do in this Christian Age. No animal sacrifices are offered during the Christian dispensation, but the spiritual sacrifices of singing, praying, observing the Lord's Supper, giving, studying the Word of God, and rendering Christian service are offered to God by each Christian. Of singing, the writer of Hebrews said, "Through Him then, let us continually offer up a sacrifice of praise to God, that is, the fruit of lips that give thanks to His name" (Hebrews 13:15). In Revelation, in apocalyptic language, the prayers of the saints on earth are described as incense being placed on the golden altar (Revelation 8:3). One of the overarching purposes of the church on earth is to "offer up spiritual sacrifices acceptable to God through Jesus Christ" (1 Peter 2:5). The writer of Hebrews pictures the door to the presence of God as being always open to Christians through the blood of Christ:

> Since therefore, brethren, we have confidence to enter the holy place by the blood of Jesus, by a new and living way which He inaugurated for us through the veil, that is, His flesh, and since we have a great priest over the house of God, let us draw near with a sincere heart in full assurance of faith, having our hearts sprinkled clean from an evil conscience and our bodies washed with pure water (Hebrews 10:19-22).

Christ Jesus has become our great, eternal High Priest, and every Christian is a priest who can come to God anytime, anywhere through Him. Our Savior has "entered the holy place once for all, having obtained eternal redemption" for us (Hebrews 9:12). High priests of the Old Testament Age offered an animal sacrifice and took the blood into the Most Holy Place for atonement for the nation once a year, but Christ went into heaven itself with the offering of Himself (Hebrews

9:24, 25). Now, through that personal sacrifice which Christ has made, He will remain our High Priest forever, thus providing for us a personal priesthood before God. Because of this, Christians have been commanded to teach God's Word throughout the world that all men may know of His saving grace (Mark 16:15, 16).

The function of an object generally suggests its identity. Because an instrument which has a long handle and a sharply curved blade on the end of it is used for hoeing, we call it a hoe. Because a little tool which has a short handle and a metal head with a flat side is used for hammering nails, we call it a hammer. Since Christians are to function as priests before God, we are not surprised that the New Testament calls us priests. Three times in the New Testament, Christians are specifically referred to as priests (Revelation 1:6; 5:10; 20:6); and at numerous others times their priesthood is implied by their function (1 Peter 2:5, 9; Hebrews 13:15).

The truth that we have been invited by the Lord to function in this world as priests of God should give us a clearer vision of the importance of our work and service. Any Old Testament priest would have a sense of significance surrounding all of his activities—for he was God's special servant, guiding His nation in worship and service before God. Even so, as God's holy priesthood today, we worship, serve, and teach in gratitude that God has given us this incomparable function on His earth.

Since we function as God's priests, we should feel a great sense of responsibility. The head of a trucking firm placed a sign over the exit gate for the truck drivers to read as they left to take their loads to different destinations. It read, "Beyond This Gate, You Represent the Company." When people saw those truck drivers, they saw the company. Since we are God's priests, we represent God in the world. Fellow priest, do we take our responsibility seriously?

CONCLUSION

Christians, then, are God's holy priesthood in the Christian Age. We have priestly access to God, we have been granted priestly privileges, and we fulfill a priestly function in the world. We have the highest honor, for we have been set apart to be Jehovah's own people. We have the highest calling, for we have been called to be holy, to be like God. We have the highest work, for we have been given the function of priests of God.

Are you a Christian? Have you allowed Christ to cleanse you of your sins and make you one of God's priests? We should want to be Christians, not only because of what a Christian receives, but also because of what a Christian is and does.

Our songs echo our interests, loyalties, and values. This is also true in heaven. What songs are being sung in heaven? Notice the song that was sung by the court of heaven when the Lamb took the book with the seven seals out of the hand of the One who occupied the throne:

> "Worthy art Thou to take the book, and to break its seals; for Thou wast slain, and didst purchase for God with Thy blood men from every tribe and tongue and people and nation. And Thou hast made them to be a kingdom and priests to our God; and they will reign upon the earth" (Revelation 5:9, 10).

If you were asked by the president of your nation to serve the nation as part of his cabinet, would you accept? Most likely. If you were asked by the mayor of your city to serve your city as its special servant, would you accept? Surely you would. God, the Creator of the universe, the One who has offered redemption to you through His Son, is asking you to come to Him and serve Him and this world as His holy priesthood. Will you accept?

QUESTIONS FOR STUDY AND DISCUSSION

1. Compare the laws for minors and the laws for adults in your nation.
2. Describe how the Jews of the first century may have been confused about which law they were under, whether the law of Moses or the new law of Christ.
3. What do you think stood out as being really different in the mind of a Jew who had become a Christian?
4. What kind of special relationship existed between God and the priest of the Old Testament?
5. How does being God's priests give us worth and significance today?
6. What does the phrase "access to God" mean?
7. List specific blessings which we enjoy as a result of having access to God.
8. How do we function as God's priests today?
9. List the Scriptures which refer to Christians as priests of God.
10. How does Revelation 5:9, 10 reflect the priesthood of believers?

11. How does one become a priest of God today?
12. Can anyone become a priest of God today?

For Preaching and Teaching Purposes: Sermon or Teaching Type: Basic pattern; deductive; textual. Subject: The church. Theme: The church as God's holy priesthood. Title: God's Holy Priesthood. Preaching or Teaching Portion: Revelation 1:5, 6. Proposition: (Declarative) The church is God's holy priesthood today. Interrogative Question or Probing Question: How? Key Word: Ways. Major Points: I. A Priestly Privilege From God; II. A Priestly Access to God; III. A Priestly Function for God. Sermonic or Teaching Objective: To persuade the Christian to live as God's priest.

13

Christs Bondservants

"But now having been freed from sin and enslaved to God, you derive your benefit, resulting in sanctification, and the outcome, eternal life" (Romans 6:22).

A few years ago I was in Modesto, California, delivering a series of evangelistic sermons. My family was with me, and a Christian family kept us in their home during two days of the meeting. They put Susan and me in a very spacious, elaborate bedroom. Our second day with them was very busy, and I could not find time for my daily exercise until after the service, at ten o'clock that night. It was late when I returned to the house after walking for an hour. All the lights were off except the one in the living room. Our host and hostess had left the door unlocked for me, so I slipped in the front door and through the house to the bedroom they had given us. On my way through, I could not help noticing that the living room had been made into a bedroom. The couch had been made into a bed, and the couple who were keeping us were sleeping on the couch. It struck me with terrific impact that these two Christians were true servants. They had given us the best bedroom they had while they used a makeshift bed in the living room! In Christian consideration, they had put us first and themselves last!

This couple, according to the New Testament, should be a miniature picture of the church. Kings and queens do not make up the church; servants do! Our Savior, the Head of the church, said, ". . . whoever wishes to be first among you shall be your slave; just as the Son of Man did not come to be served, but to serve, and to give His life a ransom for many" (Matthew 20:27, 28). No wonder Paul wrote of the followers of Christ, "Do nothing from selfishness or empty conceit, but with humility of mind let each of you regard one another as more important than himself; do not merely look out for your own personal interests, but also for the interests of others" (Philippians 2:3, 4). Peter also exhorted the church of Christ, "Act as free men, and do not use your freedom as a covering for evil, but use it as bondslaves of God" (1 Peter 2:16).

Unless we view the church as a body of servants of Christ, we will miss a key aspect of the nature of the authentic church of Christ. Intertwined in the meaning and life of the church is the concept of servanthood. The thought begins with Christ, the Founder and Head of the church, and carries through to and sets the standard for every member. Any church that claims to be Christ's church but does not see its life in the world in terms of clear, bold servanthood simply claims to be something that it is not.

Because of the paramount importance of this feature of the church, we must consider carefully how we, the church of Christ, are the servants of Christ.

IN DESIGNATION

First, we see our role as servants in our designation. That the church is made up of servants of Christ is indicated in the New Testament by the descriptive expressions used of the church. Christ obviously intended for His people to be servants, or He would not have characterized His church as He did.

He defined true greatness among His followers with a portrait of a servant: "You know that the rulers of the Gentiles lord it over them, and their great men exercise authority over them. It is not so among you, but whoever wishes to become great among you shall be your servant" (Matthew 20:25, 26). Greatness, according to Christ, is seen in terms of service rendered, not in terms of possessions owned or positions held.

In conversion to Christ, Paul pictured the sinner as becoming the servant of God and of Christ. Before conversion, we were the servants of sin, but following conversion, we are the servants of righteousness (Romans 6:17, 18). Christians do not belong to themselves but are the exclusive, personal property of God: "For you have been bought with a price: therefore glorify God in your body" (1 Corinthians 6:20). Whether we live or die, we are the Lord's: "For not one of us lives for himself, and not one dies for himself; for if we live, we live for the Lord, or if we die, we die for the Lord; therefore whether we live or die, we are the Lord's" (Romans 14:7, 8).

The concept of our being servants of God and Christ should naturally be seen in our service to one another. Accordingly, we are told to "be subject to one another in the fear of Christ" (Ephesians 5:21), not demanding our own way but always considering our brother's welfare and spiritual life. Paul wrote, "For if because of food your brother is hurt, you are no longer walking according to love. Do not destroy with your food him for whom Christ died. . . . For he who in this way serves Christ is acceptable to God and approved by men" (Romans 14:15, 18). Therefore, as Christ's servants, we have been commanded to "be devoted to one another in brotherly love" and "give preference to one another in honor" (Romans 12:10). We are also commanded, "For you were called to freedom, brethren; only do not turn your freedom into an opportunity for the flesh, but through love serve one another" (Galatians 5:13).

Christ's servants are in the world to do His bidding. They preach His gospel, not theirs; they seek to fulfill His mission, not one they have planned. With Paul they say, "For am I now seeking the favor of men, or of God? Or am I striving to please men? If I were still trying to please men, I would not be a bond-servant of Christ" (Galatians 1:10).

The story is told of a soldier in the army of Alexander the Great. The young soldier's first name was Alexander. He became guilty of wrongdoing which was totally out of character for a soldier in Alexander's mighty army. His misconduct was discovered, and he was brought before the king for judgment. Alexander asked him his name. The soldier softly said, "Alexander." The great commander looked up at him with a stern, fiery stare and said, "Soldier, either change your life or change your name!"

The church has been given a designation by the Holy Spirit of God. The question "How can the church be what Christ intended us to be in the world?" is decisively answered in the Scriptures: "Live up to your designation! Be what you are called. Be the servants of Christ."

Winston Churchill said, "The best way to create a virtue in someone is to attribute that virtue to them." God instills the virtue of servanthood in His people by attributing that virtue to us, by calling us His servants.

Obviously, before we can be servants, we must think as servants think. Let us practice servant thinking. Let us not ask, "What will I get out of this?" but ask, "How can I be of help to my brother? What does he need most to help him to grow in Christ and be strong in the faith?" Let us not ask, "Lord, what have You done for me lately?" but ask, "Lord, here am I. Send me!"

IN DESIRE

We are not only the servants of Christ in designation, but also in desire. His true church has no other ambition. Above all other aspirations, His people seek to serve Him.

Before Christ came, we had no hope and faced eternal despair. No man could have helped us. Nothing constructed by men could have saved us. All the learning of all the universities and centers of education could not have devised a way for us to be redeemed. The only prospect we had was divine intervention.

Then, God sent Christ to this earth as our divine Savior. He became fully human even though He was the second member of the Godhead. He left His place of glory as God in eternity and became one of us that He might taste of death for us (Hebrews 2:9). He selflessly laid aside His splendor of heaven and entered into the humiliation of earth. He became so completely human that He suffered in the ways all of us suffer and was subject to death even as all of us are. He did all of this so that He might exhibit a perfect life before us and lay down His life as a sin offering for us. Our guilt of sin had created a debt that only the sinless life of the divine Son of God could pay.

He did not have to spend one minute on this earth, but He came because He loved us and wanted to rescue us. He did not have to suffer one discomfort or pain, but He underwent the unimaginable pain of crucifixion to save us. Even His Father did not make Him go to the cross and die; He went voluntarily because He wanted to offer us salvation (John 10:18). His love for us had no hidden agendas—no personal, selfish plans. It contained no hypocrisy, no false pretense, but was pure and genuine.

We therefore are indebted to Jesus beyond the ability of words to express. First, we have received from Him *redemption*: "In Him we have redemption through His blood, the forgiveness of our trespasses, according to the riches of His grace" (Ephesians 1:7); ". . . you were not redeemed with perishable things like silver or gold from your futile way of life inherited from your forefathers, but with precious blood, as of a lamb unblemished and spotless, the blood of Christ" (1 Peter 1:18, 19).

Second, we have received from Him an *endowment*. Our talents and possessions are precious gifts from Him. ". . . And what do you have that you did not receive? But if you did receive it, why do you boast as if you had not received it?" (1 Corinthians 4:7).

Third, He has given us *identity*. Having been redeemed by His blood and having been endowed for His service through His grace, we are His stewards.

We belong completely to Him. We do not claim anything that we have as our own. From the hairs of our heads to the tips of our fingers to the soles of our feet, we are His property. Our only desire is to serve Him. Because of what He has done for us, we would have it no other way.

The life that we are called to live, the mission we have, and the message we preach reflect the spirit of servanthood.

The story is told of a slave girl who was to be auctioned off shortly before the American Civil War. She was in her late teens. Under other circumstances, she would have had a zest for living and would have been entering the future as one would embark upon a pleasant journey. She was a slave, however, and her eyes reflected the frustrated ambition of her soul. As she looked over the crowd that awaited an opportunity to bid for her ownership, she shuddered to think of what kind of future she might have. Soon the air was filled with the strong voice of the auctioneer as he called for bids. Higher and higher the bids rose. Finally, the bidding ceased, and a quietness hung over the crowd until the auctioneer said with awful and bone-chilling finality, "Sold!" The word shook the young woman from her stare, and she glanced over the crowd to see who was moving to the front to claim her as a possession. A middle-aged man was pushing through the crowd to the front. He stepped to the side and paid the amount that he had offered. He then turned and walked toward her. Taking her by the arm, he led her away from the crowd. Without a word to her, he took out a piece of paper and wrote across it, "On this date, I have bought you, and I have granted you your freedom." At the bottom of the page, he signed his name and then handed the document of freedom to the young lady. With her hands trembling and her body shaking with uncontrollable emotion, she hugged the paper to her breast, wondering if this could be real and not a dream. Then, after the full realization of what had happened sank in, she fell at the man's feet and said, "Sir, I'll be your servant forever—gladly, willingly, and freely."

Her picture is also a picture of the church. We were slaves of sin and destined to wretched lives of bondage to the devil, controlled and dominated by his evil impulses and desires, but Jesus bought us with His blood and set us free. We live for Him now. We have fallen at His feet and pledged our loyalty to Him in undying love and appreciation for what He has done for us.

Any Christian who does not aspire to be the servant of Christ simply has not contemplated fully what he owes Christ. Without Him we would be nothing. Draw in your mind a zero and stretch out the hole in that zero until you have a zero bigger than the earth. Only then will you have a zero that illustrates what we would be like without Christ! Without Christ we were less than nothing! A realization of what Christ has done for us compels us to express our gratitude in daily service to Him.

IN DEMONSTRATION

Third, we, the church of Christ, are the servants of Christ in demonstration. The life that we are called to live, the mission we have, and the message we preach reflect the spirit of servanthood.

Servanthood is always at the heart of the Christian life. This is true because the Christian life is the "Christ-in-us" life, and Christ was the greatest servant the world has ever seen. Paul wrote, "I have been crucified with Christ; and it is no longer I who live, but Christ lives in me; and the life which I now live in the flesh I live by faith in the Son of God, who loved me, and delivered Himself up for me" (Galatians 2:20). That being the case, it should not surprise us to see Paul living a servant life: He was selfless and sacrificing, not selfish and self-serving. He wrote to us, "Have this attitude in yourselves which was also in Christ Jesus" (Philippians 2:5). If we follow his admonition and live with the mind of Christ, we will think of others and live for others:

> ... although He existed in the form of God, [He] did not regard equality with God a thing to be grasped, but emptied Himself, taking the form of a bond-servant, and being made in the likeness of men. And being found in appearance as a man, He humbled Himself by becoming obedient to the point of death, even death on a cross (Philippians 2:6-8).

The mind of Christ was a self-emptying mind. He laid aside His heavenly glory, becoming a servant of men, His own creation, and submitted to crucifixion for the salvation of man. If we live with His mind, we can fill no other role than that of serving men.

The mission Christ has given His people cannot be implemented without servanthood. Jesus told His disciples when He sent them out on His limited commission, "Freely you received, freely give" (Matthew 10:8). When He gave to His disciples His final, worldwide commission, He mandated servanthood: "Go into all the world and preach the gospel to all creation" (Mark 16:15). For His commission to be carried out, many of us must be willing to go, leaving behind people, possessions, and cultures we hold dear; and the rest of us must be willing to give sacrificially to send those who go, giving up monies we could have spent on ourselves. The ones who are going and the ones who are sending will be fulfilling the role of servants. No one goes to the mission field to get rich, and no one gives to get rich. Both do what they do as servants of Christ.

The message we preach is not our own. We did not write the letter; we are only public servants who deliver the letter Christ has written. We see to it that the message He has sent is not distorted or obscured. We have no orders from our King to rewrite it; we are commanded to see to it that it is accurately delivered. We know that the world is lost without this message. Therefore, out of compassion and lovingkindness, we herald His message in every conceivable way—through the printed page, on radio and T.V., from pulpits, through personal contacts, and in daily example. We put His message first—even above our own personal convenience and dreams. For its preaching, we give our talents, our money, our time, our minds, our hands, our feet—yes, even our very hearts.

Our King is so different from all other kings! Although He is the King of kings, the Creator and Sustainer of all the universe, He lived among us as a servant. This truth especially shines through the event of Jesus' washing His disciples' feet at the Last Supper (John 13:1-16). When an earthly king comes among us, people bow before him and reach out to touch him. When the pope comes out among his people, they bow before him and seek to kiss his hand. When Christ, however, was with His disciples the night before His death, He filled a basin with water and washed their feet.

Why did He do it? Not because He had to or because no one else would. He did not do it just because He knew that an illustration would be valuable to His disciples. He did it because of who He is— He is the Son of God and the servant of men. He came as a servant, He lived as a servant, and He died as a servant. Serving others was as natural to Him as walking and eating. Because of who we are, He calls His followers to the same kind of life:

> "You call Me Teacher and Lord; and you are right, for so I am. If I then, the Lord and the Teacher, washed your feet, you also ought to wash one another's feet. For I gave you an example that you also should do as I did to you. Truly, truly, I say to you, a slave is not greater than his master; neither is one who is sent greater than the one who sent him" (John 13:13-16).

We are to walk as Jesus walked. Servanthood is so interwoven into the Christian's life, mission, and message that we cannot engage in genuine Christian living without centering our thoughts on service to others.

If you are wondering how you can live a servant's life, just do what Christ asked you to do. You will find that you cannot carry out His will without being a servant. You cannot teach others His gospel the way He asked you to unless you are a servant; you cannot care for the poor, as He said to do it, without being a servant; you cannot fulfill the mission He gave you without the heart of a servant.

CONCLUSION

The New Testament makes it clear that the church is composed of servants of Christ. We are servants in designation, in desire, and in demonstration. The ground at the foot of the cross is level. No servant is elevated above another, and no servant is placed beneath another. We are all just servants.

Clovis Chappell told of his crossing the ocean on a ship. It was his first time to take a trip of this kind, and the trip was too much for him. He became so seasick that he could hardly stand up. He said his sleeping place was the top bunk, and being in that top bunk was unbearable to him. He said he thought he was going to die. The man who had the bunk immediately below him, a complete stranger to him, saw how sick he was and, with a compassion which seemed as natural to him as breathing, suggested that they switch bunks. He then began to assist him as a nurse would a patient. Without any request from Chappell, he scurried about tending to his needs with tender concern. Mr. Chappell said that he continued to remember that man through the years because servanthood to him was a way of life. He must have thought as a servant thinks, and thus, wherever he was, whether at home or abroad, he lived as a servant.

Christ's followers should find being servants as natural as combing their hair or taking a walk, as natural as drinking a glass of water or eating a meal. Our lives have been converted from self-centeredness to Son-centeredness, and this can mean only one thing—servanthood.

Christ's invitation has ever been for sinners to come to salvation and servanthood. He says to us "come" (Matthew 11:28, 29) and "go" (Matthew 28:19, 20). He will receive anyone who will come, but He will leave no one as he is when he comes. He receives us as sinners, but He transforms us into servants of men. His true church, therefore, is made up of servants of the Servant.

Are you a servant of Christ?

QUESTIONS FOR STUDY
AND DISCUSSION

1. Briefly define "servant."
2. Discuss the statement "We are free yet slaves of Christ."
3. Explain how servanthood leads to greatness, according to Christ (Matthew 20:25, 26).
4. What does it mean to be a "servant of righteousness"?
5. Why do we belong to Christ?
6. What does it mean to be "subject" to one another in the fear of Christ?
7. How could one destroy his brother with food?
8. What does it mean to be "devoted to one another in brotherly love"?
9. Why should the church desire to be the servants of Christ?
10. In what three ways are we indebted to Christ?
11. Explain the Christian life as the "Christ-in-us" life.
12. What is a self-emptying mind?
13. Can the mission Christ has given us be implemented without servanthood?

14. What was Christ seeking to teach when He washed the disciples' feet?
15. What is meant by the expression "The ground at the foot of the cross is level"?

For Preaching and Teaching Purposes: Sermon or Teaching Type: Basic pattern; deductive; topical. Subject: The church. Theme: Christ's servants. Title: Christ's Bondservants. Preaching or Teaching Portion: None. Proposition: (Declarative) We are the servants of Christ. Interrogative Question or Probing Question: How? Key Word: Ways. Major Points: I. In Designation; II. In Desire; III. In Demonstration. Sermonic or Teaching Objective: To persuade Christians to live as the servants of Christ.

Epilogue

If You Are on the Outside Looking In

"And the Spirit and the bride say, 'Come.' And let the one who hears say, 'Come.' And let the one who is thirsty come; let the one who wishes take the water of life without cost" (Revelation 22:17).

Where are you? Are you in Christ or outside of Him? You may have heard the refrain "I'd rather be on the inside looking out, than on the outside looking in." If the verse is referring to a prison, I would not agree with it—I would rather be on the outside looking in, not on the inside looking out! If the subject is the church of Christ, however, I could sing the song without any reservations—I want to be on the inside looking out!

After considering the Scriptures of the New Testament that relate to the church, surely you believe as I do. Who could ponder the design that God has for "the church" and not long to be a part of it, not yearn to be on the inside looking out?

If you are on the outside of the church looking in, where do you go from here? How can you enter the church, or become a member of Christ's body?

Jesus adds us to His church. You cannot join it in the secular sense of the word; however, He will gladly add you to it (Acts 2:47) as He did those first-century people who received His Word and obeyed it. They believed in the Jesus portrayed to them in the Word (Acts 2:41; Romans 10:17), they repented of their sins as they made a resolute commitment to follow Christ in daily living (Acts 17:30, 31), they confessed Jesus as God's Son with their lips, affirming the faith in Christ which they had in their hearts (Romans 10:10), and they were baptized by immersion into Christ for the forgiveness of their sins (Romans 6:3; Acts 2:38; 22:16). When they obeyed the Word preached to them, Christ added them to His church (Acts 2:47). Do what they did, and Christ will do for you what He did for them. The same gospel that made them Christians in the first century will make you a Christian today.

If you know how to become a Christian but do not know which step to take first, call a gospel preacher near you. You may contact him by calling the number listed for the church of Christ in your telephone directory. He will be glad to assist you. Do not settle for any plan of salvation other than the one the Master has given us through His inspired Word. Give your whole heart to Christ as you obey His Word, and you can be assured that He will add you to His body. Then, after your obedience to Christ, live for Him as His church. If there is no church of Christ near you, write the address given on the facing page, and we will help you find someone in your area to assist you.

If you would like to study more about the church Jesus built, write to the address on the facing page, and we will enroll you in a free Bible correspondence course. Please do not remain on the outside looking in; let Christ add you to His glorious church so that you might enjoy the abundant life now and eternal life in the world to come.

A Free Bible Study

If you would like to study more about the church in the New Testament, send your name and your complete mailing address to the address below. You will be contacted through the mail by a teacher who will study with you through a Bible correspondence course. As you work to complete this course, you will explore the Word of God and gain a better understanding of the New Testament and the church that Christ established.

World Bible School Correspondence Course
Truth for Today
202 S. Locust
Searcy, AR 72143
Phone: (501) 268-7588

Appendix 1

The Divine Action
Of Conversion

"Everything ultimately depends upon God's grace. His grace is the source of salvation and the sustaining power and motivation of salvation."

What does God do for a sinner when he chooses to become a Christian? What divine actions does He take as He brings the sinner into salvation? If we can understand what God does for us when we enter the body of Christ, or the church, our appreciation for this "special beginning" which we call "conversion to Christ" will be increased immeasurably.

Study carefully this list of actions which God takes when one becomes a Christian. You will find under the designation of each action at least one verse of Scripture which indicates that God does in fact take this action. In some cases, numerous verses could have been cited, but one verse is sufficient to prove that the action does occur. You will notice that, according to this list, forty-two different and/or related actions are taken by our gracious God when one becomes a Christian. Obviously, some of these designations overlap and are simply a different way of saying the same thing. In this context, fine lines of distinction have not been drawn between actions. The purpose of this list is to bring before us the Scriptures which explain God's actions as He ushers us into His family, the church. We will see, almost at a glance, the scope of those actions.

(1) **We are given Christ as our Savior.**
Titus 3:5, 6
"He saved us, . . . according to His mercy, by the washing of regeneration and renewing by the Holy Spirit, whom He poured out upon us richly through Jesus Christ our Savior."

(2) **We are brought into the one body.**
1 Corinthians 12:13
"For by one Spirit we were all baptized into one body, whether Jews or Greeks, whether slaves or free, and we were all made to drink of one Spirit."

(3) **We are clothed with Christ.**
Galatians 3:27
"For all of you who were baptized into Christ have clothed yourselves with Christ."

(4) **We receive the benefits of Christ's death.**
Romans 6:3
"Or do you not know that all of us who have been baptized into Christ Jesus have been baptized into His death?"

(5) **We are born of God.**
1 John 5:1
"Whoever believes that Jesus is the Christ is

born of God; and whoever loves the Father
loves the child born of Him."

(6) **We are washed in the blood of Christ.**
Revelation 1:5, 6
". . . To Him who loves us, and released us from
our sins by His [Christ's] blood, . . . to Him be
the glory and the dominion forever and ever.
Amen."

(7) **We are saved.**
Mark 16:16
"'He who has believed and has been baptized
shall be saved; but he who has disbelieved
shall be condemned.'"

(8) **We are forgiven of sin.**
Colossians 1:13, 14
"For He delivered us from the domain of darkness, and transferred us to the kingdom of His
beloved Son, in whom we have redemption,
the forgiveness of sins."

(9) **We are made righteous or just in God's sight.**
Romans 3:23, 24
"For all have sinned and fall short of the glory
of God, being justified as a gift by His grace
through the redemption which is in Christ
Jesus."

(10) **We are redeemed.**
Ephesians 1:7
"In Him we have redemption through His
blood, the forgiveness of our trespasses, according to the riches of His grace."

(11) **We are delivered from the slavery to sin.**
Romans 6:17, 18
"But thanks be to God that though you were slaves of sin, you became obedient from the heart to that form of teaching to which you were committed, and having been freed from sin, you became slaves of righteousness."

(12) **We are set apart or sanctified.**
1 Corinthians 6:11
"And such were some of you; but you were washed, but you were sanctified, but you were justified in the name of the Lord Jesus Christ, and in the Spirit of our God."

(13) **We are adopted as children of God.**
Ephesians 1:5
"He predestined us to adoption as sons through Jesus Christ to Himself, according to the kind intention of His will."

(14) **We are made spiritually alive.**
Ephesians 2:5
"Even when we were dead in our transgressions, [God] made us alive together with Christ (by grace you have been saved)."

(15) **We are placed in Christ.**
Ephesians 2:6
"And [God] raised us up with Him, and seated us with Him in the heavenly places, in Christ Jesus."

(16) **We are recipients of God's grace.**

Ephesians 2:8, 9
"For by grace you have been saved through faith; and that not of yourselves, it is the gift of God; not as a result of works, that no one should boast."

(17) **We are reconciled to God.**
Colossians 1:19, 20
"For it was the Father's good pleasure for all the fulness to dwell in Him, and through Him to reconcile all things to Himself, having made peace through the blood of His cross; . . ."

(18) **We are made one in Christ.**
Ephesians 2:14-16
"For He Himself is our peace, who made both groups into one, and broke down the barrier of the dividing wall, . . . that in Himself He might make the two into one new man, thus establishing peace, and might reconcile them both in one body to God through the cross, . . ."

(19) **We are made new creatures.**
2 Corinthians 5:17
"Therefore if any man is in Christ, he is a new creature; the old things passed away; behold, new things have come."

(20) **We are made heirs of God.**
Romans 8:17
"And if children, heirs also, heirs of God and fellow heirs with Christ, if indeed we suffer with Him in order that we may also be glorified with Him."

(21) **We are indwelt by Deity.**

> **Indwelt by the Spirit**
> Galatians 4:6
> "And because you are sons, God has sent
> forth the Spirit of His Son into our hearts,
> crying, 'Abba! Father!'"

> **Indwelt by God**
> 1 John 4:15
> "Whoever confesses that Jesus is the Son
> of God, God abides in him, and he in
> God."

> **Indwelt by Christ**
> John 14:23
> "Jesus answered and said to him, 'If any-
> one loves Me, he will keep My word; and
> My Father will love him, and We will
> come to him, and make Our abode with
> him.'"

(22) **We are given access to all spiritual blessings.**
Ephesians 1:3
"Blessed be the God and Father of our Lord
Jesus Christ, who has blessed us with every
spiritual blessing in the heavenly places in
Christ."

(23) **We are made citizens of the kingdom of God.**
John 3:3
"Jesus answered and said to him, 'Truly, truly,
I say to you, unless one is born again, he cannot
see the kingdom of God.'"

(24) **We are brought out of condemnation.**
Romans 8:1
"There is therefore now no condemnation for those who are in Christ Jesus."

(25) **We are given fellowship with God, Christ, and the Spirit.**
1 John 1:3
"What we have seen and heard we proclaim to you also, that you also may have fellowship with us; and indeed our fellowship is with the Father, and with His Son Jesus Christ."

(26) **We enter continual cleansing.**
1 John 1:7
"But if we walk in the light as He Himself is in the light, we have fellowship with one another, and the blood of Jesus His Son cleanses us from all sin."

(27) **We are enabled to become partakers of divine nature.**
2 Peter 1:4
"For by these He has granted to us His precious and magnificent promises, in order that by them you might become partakers of the divine nature, having escaped the corruption that is in the world by lust."

(28) **We are given living hope.**
1 Peter 1:3
"Blessed be the God and Father of our Lord Jesus Christ, who according to His great mercy has caused us to be born again to a living hope

through the resurrection of Jesus Christ from the dead."

(29) We are brought under God's protection.
1 Peter 1:3-5
"Blessed be the God and Father of our Lord Jesus Christ, who according to His great mercy has caused us to be born again ... to obtain an inheritance which is imperishable and undefiled and will not fade away, reserved in heaven for you, who are protected by the power of God through faith for a salvation ready to be revealed in the last time."

(30) We are given legal peace with God.
Romans 5:1
"Therefore having been justified by faith, we have peace with God through our Lord Jesus Christ."

(31) We are given access to God's daily peace.
Philippians 4:7
"And the peace of God, which surpasses all comprehension, shall guard your hearts and your minds in Christ Jesus."

(32) We are given Christ as our Advocate.
1 John 2:1
"My little children, I am writing these things to you that you may not sin. And if anyone sins, we have an Advocate with the Father, Jesus Christ the righteous."

(33) We are given eternal life.

1 John 5:12
"He who has the Son has the life; he who does not have the Son of God does not have the life."

(34) **We are granted a taste of the heavenly gift.**
Hebrews 6:4-6
"For in the case of those who have once been enlightened and have tasted of the heavenly gift and have been made partakers of the Holy Spirit, and have tasted the good word of God and the powers of the age to come, . . ."

(35) **Our names are enrolled in heaven.**
Luke 10:20
"'Nevertheless do not rejoice in this, that the spirits are subject to you, but rejoice that your names are recorded in heaven.'"

(36) **We become the chosen of God.**
Ephesians 1:4
"Just as He chose us in Him before the foundation of the world, that we should be holy and blameless before Him. . . ."

(37) **Our hearts are purified by faith.**
Acts 15:9
"And He made no distinction between us and them, cleansing their hearts by faith."

(38) **Our consciences are cleansed from dead works.**
Hebrews 10:22
"Let us draw near with a sincere heart in full assurance of faith, having our hearts sprinkled

clean from an evil conscience and our bodies washed with pure water."

(39) **We are brought nigh to God and Christ.**
Ephesians 2:13
"But now in Christ Jesus you who formerly were far off have been brought near by the blood of Christ."

(40) **We are spiritually circumcised from the old man of sin.**
Colossians 2:11, 12
"And in Him you were also circumcised with a circumcision made without hands, in the removal of the body of the flesh by the circumcision of Christ; having been buried with Him in baptism, in which you were also raised up with Him through faith in the working of God, who raised Him from the dead."

(41) **We are sealed with the Holy Spirit of promise.**
Ephesians 1:13
"In Him, you also, after listening to the message of truth, the gospel of your salvation—having also believed, you were sealed in Him with the Holy Spirit of promise."

(42) **Christ is made known to us.**
John 14:21
"'He who has My commandments and keeps them, he it is who loves Me; and he who loves Me shall be loved by My Father, and I will love him, and will disclose Myself to him.'"

Appendix 2

The Human Action Of Conversion

"All agree that a response must be made to receive the grace of God. Some disagree on the response that should be made. Is there a solution? Yes. We must let the Bible tell us what response to make."

What actions must a sinner take to become a Christian? What should he do to receive salvation and the grace of God?

The New Testament's instructions on how to become a Christian can be called "actions" or "steps." These responses to the gospel constitute the means by which a sinner becomes a recipient of the saving, divine work of God. The sinner is not passive in the salvation process. It is true that God, the source of our salvation, saves him, but the sinner must *receive* God's salvation and walk in it.

Study carefully this list of actions. You will find listed under each action those Scriptures which confirm that this action is to be taken. Fourteen different steps and/or actions must be taken to receive Christ's redemption, according to this list. The list is divided into two parts—the general responses and the specific ones. Obviously, overlapping in the responses occurs.

Sometimes an individual or specific step is used by an inspired writer as a synecdoche, as he makes a part stand for the whole. For example, the word "faith" is often used for the totality of the human response needed for salvation. When this is done, the writer has used "faith" as a summary of all the human obedience which is necessary. When an action is so used, the action figuratively includes all the other actions that are to be taken by a sinner. The other actions are comprehended in the one action. Watch for verses which use one action in this way.

General Responses

(1) **We are to come to Christ.**
Matthew 11:28-30
"'Come to Me, all who are weary and heavy-laden, and I will give you rest. Take My yoke upon you, and learn from Me, for I am gentle and humble in heart; and you shall find rest for your souls. For My yoke is easy, and My load is light.'"

Revelation 22:17
"And the Spirit and the bride say, 'Come.' And let the one who hears say, 'Come.' And let the one who is thirsty come; let the one who wishes take the water of life without cost."

(2) **We are to save ourselves.**
Acts 2:40
"And with many other words he solemnly

testified and kept on exhorting them, saying, 'Be saved from this perverse generation!'"

(3) We are to obey.
Romans 6:17, 18
"But thanks be to God that though you were slaves of sin, you became obedient from the heart to that form of teaching to which you were committed, and having been freed from sin, you became slaves of righteousness."

(4) We are to receive the Word.
Acts 2:41
"So then, those who had received his word were baptized; and there were added that day about three thousand souls."

(5) We are to abide in the Word.
John 8:31, 32
"Jesus therefore was saying to those Jews who had believed Him, 'If you abide in My word, then you are truly disciples of Mine; and you shall know the truth, and the truth shall make you free.'"

(6) We are to die to sin.
Romans 6:1, 2
"What shall we say then? Are we to continue in sin that grace might increase? May it never be! How shall we who died to sin still live in it?"

(7) We are to put on the new man.
Colossians 3:10
"And [you] have put on the new self who is

being renewed to a true knowledge according
to the image of the One who created him."

Specific Responses

(1) **We are to listen to God's Word.**
Acts 18:8
"And Crispus, the leader of the synagogue,
believed in the Lord with all his household,
and many of the Corinthians when they heard
were believing and being baptized."

Romans 10:17
"So faith comes from hearing, and hearing by
the word of Christ."

By taking heed to what we hear
Acts 17:11
"Now these were more noble-minded than
those in Thessalonica, for they received
the word with great eagerness, examining
the Scriptures daily, to see whether these
things were so."

1 Thessalonians 5:21
"But examine everything carefully; hold
fast to that which is good."

By taking heed to how we hear
Matthew 7:24
"'Therefore everyone who hears these
words of Mine, and acts upon them, may
be compared to a wise man, who built his
house upon the rock.'"

Matthew 13:9
"'He who has ears, let him hear.'"

(2) **We are to believe.**
Romans 5:1
"Therefore having been justified by faith, we have peace with God through our Lord Jesus Christ."

In God
Hebrews 11:6
"And without faith it is impossible to please Him, for he who comes to God must believe that He is, and that He is a rewarder of those who seek Him."

In Christ
John 3:16
"'For God so loved the world, that He gave His only begotten Son, that whoever believes in Him should not perish, but have eternal life.'"

(3) **We are to repent.**
Acts 11:18
"And when they heard this, they quieted down, and glorified God, saying, 'Well then, God has granted to the Gentiles also the repentance that leads to life.'"

Acts 17:30
"Therefore having overlooked the times of ignorance, God is now declaring to men that all everywhere should repent."

2 Peter 3:9
"The Lord is not slow about His promise, as some count slowness, but is patient toward you, not wishing for any to perish but for all to come to repentance."

(4) We are to turn again.
Acts 2:38
"And Peter said to them, 'Repent, and let each of you be baptized in the name of Jesus Christ for the forgiveness of your sins; and you shall receive the gift of the Holy Spirit.'"

Acts 3:19
"Repent therefore and return, that your sins may be wiped away, in order that times of refreshing may come from the presence of the Lord."

(5) We are to confess Christ.
Romans 10:10
"For with the heart man believes, resulting in righteousness, and with the mouth he confesses, resulting in salvation."

1 John 4:15
"Whoever confesses that Jesus is the Son of God, God abides in him, and he in God."

(6) We are to be baptized.
Acts 22:16
"'And now why do you delay? Arise, and be baptized, and wash away your sins, calling on His name.'"

1 Peter 3:21, 22:
"And corresponding to that, baptism now saves you—not the removal of dirt from the flesh, but an appeal to God for a good conscience—through the resurrection of Jesus Christ, who is at the right hand of God, having gone into heaven, after angels and authorities and powers had been subjected to Him."

(7) **We are to call upon God.**
Acts 2:21
"'And it shall be, that everyone who calls on the name of the Lord shall be saved.'"

Acts 22:16
"'And now why do you delay? Arise, and be baptized, and wash away your sins, calling on His name.'"

Appendix 3

The "In Christ" Phrase

"Christ is the redeemed man's new environment. He has been lifted out of the cramping restrictions of his earthly lot into a totally different sphere, the sphere of Christ. He has been transplanted into a new soil and a new climate, and both soil and climate are Christ. His spirit is breathing a nobler element. He is moving on a loftier plane."[1]

No thorough study of the church would be complete without a careful analysis of the "in Christ" phrase and its equivalents in the New Testament. The phrase appears 119 times in the Nestle's Greek text of the New Testament (if 1 Thessalonians 4:14 is not counted). Primarily, it is found in the writings of Paul, but it is also found in 1 Peter (3:16; 5:10; 5:14), 1 John (2:27, 28; 3:24; 4:13; 5:11, 20), and Revelation (14:13).

The phrase is used in different forms in the New Testament, specifically these: "in Christ," "in Christ

---

[1]James S. Stewart, *A Man in Christ* (London: Hodder and Stoughton, 1947), 157.

Jesus," "in Christ Jesus our Lord," "in the Lord Jesus Christ," "in the Lord Jesus," "in the Lord," "in Jesus," "in Him," "into Him," "in whom," "in His Son," and "in His Son Jesus Christ." The concept of being "in Christ" is also reflected in references to "the body of Christ," "Christ's body," "His body," "the body," and "one body," with sixteen occurrences of these phrases in the New Testament. The "in Christ" phrase does not actually appear in the Gospels; however, a foreshadowing of it is found one time in John 15:5 in the phrase "in Me."

The purpose of this study is to provide a list which includes only the New Testament verses which refer to being in the spiritual body of Christ. Phrases regarding believing "in Him" or "on Him" appear many times in the Gospels, but these phrases have not been included in this list. Those phrases, it is believed, should be covered in a separate study. Neither does the list include the phrase "in God," or similar phrases, such as appears in Acts 17:28.

By definition, the "in Christ" phrase, in its many different forms, designates the sphere of being in union with Christ, the sphere encompassed by the phrases "the church" (Ephesians 1:21, 22) and "the body of Christ" (Ephesians 4:12), where all spiritual blessings are provided for the redeemed.

Study carefully the different forms of this phrase, which are italicized for easy recognition. As you study them, notice the Christian's position and condition "in Christ" and the magnificent spiritual blessings which are enjoyed "in Him."

The New American Standard translation of the Scriptures has been quoted in the formulation of this list.

"In Me" (1)

John 15:5
"I am the vine, you are the branches; he who abides *in Me*, and I in him, he bears much fruit; for apart from Me you can do nothing."

"In Christ" (30)

Romans 9:1
"I am telling the truth *in Christ*, I am not lying, my conscience bearing me witness in the Holy Spirit."

Romans 12:5
"So we, who are many, are one body *in Christ*, and individually members one of another."

Romans 16:7
"Greet Andronicus and Junias, my kinsmen, and my fellow prisoners, who are outstanding among the apostles, who also were *in Christ* before me."

Romans 16:9
"Greet Urbanus, our fellow worker *in Christ*, and Stachys my beloved."

Romans 16:10
"Greet Apelles, the approved *in Christ*. Greet those who are of the household of Aristobulus."

1 Corinthians 3:1
"And I, brethren, could not speak to you as to spiritual men, but as to men of flesh, as to babes *in Christ*."

1 Corinthians 4:10
"We are fools for Christ's sake, but you are prudent *in*

Christ; we are weak, but you are strong; you are distinguished, but we are without honor."

1 Corinthians 4:15
"For if you were to have countless tutors *in Christ,* yet you would not have many fathers; for in Christ Jesus I became your father through the gospel."

1 Corinthians 4:17
"For this reason I have sent to you Timothy, who is my beloved and faithful child in the Lord, and he will remind you of my ways which are *in Christ,* just as I teach everywhere in every church."

1 Corinthians 15:17, 18
"And if Christ has not been raised, your faith is worthless; you are still in your sins. Then those also who have fallen asleep *in Christ* have perished."

1 Corinthians 15:19
"If we have hoped *in Christ* in this life only, we are of all men most to be pitied."

2 Corinthians 1:21
"Now He who establishes us with you *in Christ*[2] and anointed us is God."

2 Corinthians 2:17
"For we are not like many, peddling the word of God, but as from sincerity, but as from God, we speak *in Christ* in the sight of God."

---

[2]The Nestle's Greek text reads "into Christ."

2 Corinthians 3:14
"But their minds were hardened; for until this very day at the reading of the old covenant the same veil remains unlifted, because it is removed *in Christ*."

2 Corinthians 5:17
"Therefore if any man is *in Christ*, he is a new creature; the old things passed away; behold, new things have come."

2 Corinthians 5:19
"... God was *in Christ* reconciling the world to Himself, not counting their trespasses against them, and He has committed to us the word of reconciliation."

2 Corinthians 12:2
"I know a man *in Christ* who fourteen years ago— whether in the body I do not know, or out of the body I do not know, God knows—such a man was caught up to the third heaven."

2 Corinthians 12:19
"All this time you have been thinking that we are defending ourselves to you. Actually, it is in the sight of God that we have been speaking *in Christ*; and all for your upbuilding, beloved."

Galatians 1:22
"And I was still unknown by sight to the churches of Judea which were *in Christ*."

Galatians 2:17
"But if, while seeking to be justified *in Christ*, we ourselves have also been found sinners, is Christ then a minister of sin? May it never be!"

Ephesians 1:3
"Blessed be the God and Father of our Lord Jesus Christ, who has blessed us with every spiritual blessing in the heavenly places *in Christ*."

Ephesians 4:32
"And be kind to one another, tender-hearted, forgiving each other, just as God *in Christ* also has forgiven you."

Philippians 2:1, 2
"If therefore there is any encouragement *in Christ*, . . . make my joy complete by being of the same mind, maintaining the same love, united in spirit, intent on one purpose."

Colossians 1:2
"To the saints and faithful brethren *in Christ* who are at Colossae: Grace to you and peace from God our Father."

Colossians 1:28
"And we proclaim Him, admonishing every man and teaching every man with all wisdom, that we may present every man complete *in Christ*."

1 Thessalonians 4:16
"For the Lord Himself will descend from heaven with a shout, with the voice of the archangel, and with the trumpet of God; and the dead *in Christ* shall rise first."

Philemon 1:20
"Yes, brother, let me benefit from you in the Lord; refresh my heart *in Christ*."

1 Peter 3:16
"And keep a good conscience so that in the thing in which you are slandered, those who revile your good behavior *in Christ* may be put to shame."

1 Peter 5:10
"And after you have suffered for a little while, the God of all grace, who called you to His eternal glory *in Christ*, will Himself perfect, confirm, strengthen and establish you."

1 Peter 5:14
"Greet one another with a kiss of love. Peace be to you all who are *in Christ*."

"In Christ" (5)[3]
1 Corinthians 15:22
"For as in Adam all die, so also *in Christ* all shall be made alive."

2 Corinthians 2:14
"But thanks be to God, who always leads us in His triumph *in Christ*, and manifests through us the sweet aroma of the knowledge of Him in every place."

Ephesians 1:9, 10
"He made known to us the mystery of His will, according to His kind intention which He purposed in Him with a view to an administration suitable to the fulness of the times, that is, the summing up of all things *in Christ*, . . ."

---

[3]According to Nestle's Greek text, the passages in this section actually say "in the Christ."

Ephesians 1:11, 12
"Also we have obtained an inheritance, having been predestined according to His purpose who works all things after the counsel of His will, to the end that we who were the first to hope *in Christ* should be to the praise of His glory."

Ephesians 1:19, 20
". . . These are in accordance with the working of the strength of His might which He brought about *in Christ*, when He raised Him from the dead, and seated Him at His right hand in the heavenly places."

"In Christ Jesus" (42)

Romans 3:23, 24
"For all have sinned and fall short of the glory of God, being justified as a gift by His grace through the redemption which is *in Christ Jesus*."

Romans 6:11
"Even so consider yourselves to be dead to sin, but alive to God *in Christ Jesus*."

Romans 6:23
"For the wages of sin is death, but the free gift of God is eternal life *in Christ Jesus* our Lord."

Romans 8:1
"There is therefore now no condemnation for those who are *in Christ Jesus*."

Romans 8:2
"For the law of the Spirit of life *in Christ Jesus* has set you free from the law of sin and of death."

Romans 15:17
"Therefore *in Christ Jesus* I have found reason for boasting in things pertaining to God."

Romans 16:3
"Greet Prisca and Aquila, my fellow workers *in Christ Jesus.*"

1 Corinthians 1:2
"To the church of God which is at Corinth, to those who have been sanctified *in Christ Jesus*, saints by calling, with all who in every place call upon the name of our Lord Jesus Christ, their Lord and ours."

1 Corinthians 1:4
"I thank my God always concerning you, for the grace of God which was given you *in Christ Jesus.*"

1 Corinthians 1:30
"But by His doing you are *in Christ Jesus*, who became to us wisdom from God, and righteousness and sanctification, and redemption."

1 Corinthians 4:15
"For if you were to have countless tutors in Christ, yet you would not have many fathers; for *in Christ Jesus* I became your father through the gospel."

1 Corinthians 16:24
"My love be with you all *in Christ Jesus*. Amen."

Galatians 2:4
"But it was because of the false brethren who had sneaked in to spy out our liberty which we have *in Christ Jesus*, in order to bring us into bondage."

Galatians 3:13, 14
"Christ redeemed us from the curse of the Law, . . . in order that *in Christ Jesus* the blessing of Abraham might come to the Gentiles, . . ."

Galatians 3:28
"There is neither Jew nor Greek, there is neither slave nor free man, there is neither male nor female; for you are all one *in Christ Jesus*."

Galatians 5:6
"For *in Christ Jesus* neither circumcision nor uncircumcision means anything, but faith working through love."

Ephesians 1:1
"Paul, an apostle of Christ Jesus by the will of God, to the saints who are at Ephesus, and who are faithful *in Christ Jesus*."

Ephesians 2:4-7
"But God, . . . made us alive together with Christ . . . , and raised us up with Him, and seated us with Him in the heavenly places, *in Christ Jesus*, in order that in the ages to come He might show the surpassing riches of His grace in kindness toward us *in Christ Jesus*."

Ephesians 2:10
"For we are His workmanship, created *in Christ Jesus* for good works, which God prepared beforehand, that we should walk in them."

Ephesians 2:13
"But now *in Christ Jesus* you who formerly were far off have been brought near by the blood of Christ."

Ephesians 3:6
". . . the Gentiles are fellow heirs and fellow members of the body, and fellow partakers of the promise *in Christ Jesus* through the gospel."

Ephesians 3:11
"This was in accordance with the eternal purpose which He carried out *in Christ Jesus*[4] our Lord."

Ephesians 3:21
"To Him be the glory in the church and *in Christ Jesus* to all generations forever and ever. Amen."

Philippians 1:1
"Paul and Timothy, bond-servants of Christ Jesus, to all the saints *in Christ Jesus* who are in Philippi, including the overseers and deacons."

Philippians 1:26
"So that your proud confidence in me may abound *in Christ Jesus* through my coming to you again."

Philippians 3:3
"For we are the true circumcision, who worship in the Spirit of God and glory *in Christ Jesus* and put no confidence in the flesh."

Philippians 3:14
"I press on toward the goal for the prize of the upward call of God *in Christ Jesus*."

Philippians 4:7
"And the peace of God, which surpasses all compre-

---

[4]The Nestle's Greek text has "in the Christ Jesus."

hension, shall guard your hearts and your minds *in Christ Jesus*."

Philippians 4:19
"And my God shall supply all your needs according to His riches in glory *in Christ Jesus*."

Philippians 4:21
"Greet every saint *in Christ Jesus*. The brethren who are with me greet you."

1 Thessalonians 2:14
"For you, brethren, became imitators of the churches of God *in Christ Jesus* that are in Judea, for you also endured the same sufferings at the hands of your own countrymen, even as they did from the Jews."

1 Thessalonians 5:18
"In everything give thanks; for this is God's will for you *in Christ Jesus*."

1 Timothy 1:14
"And the grace of our Lord was more than abundant, with the faith and love which are found *in Christ Jesus*."

2 Timothy 1:1, 2
"Paul, an apostle of Christ Jesus by the will of God, according to the promise of life *in Christ Jesus*, to Timothy, . . . "

2 Timothy 1:9
". . . [God] has saved us, and called us with a holy calling, not according to our works, but according to His own purpose and grace which was granted us *in Christ Jesus* from all eternity."

2 Timothy 1:13
"Retain the standard of sound words which you have
heard from me, in the faith and love which are *in Christ
Jesus*."

2 Timothy 2:1
"You therefore, my son, be strong in the grace that is *in
Christ Jesus*."

2 Timothy 2:10
"For this reason I endure all things for the sake of those
who are chosen, that they also may obtain the salvation
which is *in Christ Jesus* and with it eternal glory."

2 Timothy 3:12
"And indeed, all who desire to live godly *in Christ Jesus*
will be persecuted."

2 Timothy 3:15
". . . from childhood you have known the sacred
writings which are able to give you the wisdom that
leads to salvation through faith which is *in Christ
Jesus*."

Philemon 23
"Epaphras, my fellow prisoner *in Christ Jesus*, greets
you."

"In Christ Jesus our Lord" (1)
Romans 8:39
"Nor height, nor depth, nor any other created thing,
shall be able to separate us from the love of God, which
is *in Christ Jesus our Lord*."

"In the Lord Jesus Christ" (3)
1 Thessalonians 1:1
"Paul and Silvanus and Timothy to the church of the Thessalonians *in* God the Father and *the Lord Jesus Christ*: Grace to you and peace."

2 Thessalonians 1:1
"Paul and Silvanus and Timothy to the church of the Thessalonians *in* God our Father and *the Lord Jesus Christ*."

2 Thessalonians 3:12
"Now such persons we command and exhort *in the Lord Jesus Christ* to work in quiet fashion and eat their own bread."

"In the Lord Jesus" (1)
Romans 14:14
"I know and am convinced *in the Lord Jesus* that nothing is unclean in itself; but to him who thinks anything to be unclean, to him it is unclean."

"In the Lord" (3)
1 Corinthians 4:17
"For this reason I have sent to you Timothy, who is my beloved and faithful child *in the Lord*, and he will remind you of my ways which are in Christ, just as I teach everywhere in every church."

2 Corinthians 2:12
"Now when I came to Troas for the gospel of Christ . . . a door was opened for me *in the Lord*."

Revelation 14:13
"And I heard a voice from heaven, saying, 'Write,

"Blessed are the dead who die *in the Lord* from now on!"' 'Yes,' says the Spirit, 'that they may rest from their labors, for their deeds follow with them.'"

"In Jesus" (1)
Ephesians 4:20, 21
"But you did not learn Christ in this way, if indeed you have heard Him and have been taught in Him, just as truth is *in Jesus*."

1 Thessalonians 4:14
"For if we believe that Jesus died and rose again, even so God will bring with Him those who have fallen asleep *in Jesus*."[5]

"In Him" (20)
2 Corinthians 1:19
"For the Son of God, Christ Jesus, who was preached among you by us—by me and Silvanus and Timothy—was not yes and no, but is yes *in Him*."

2 Corinthians 1:20
"For as many as may be the promises of God, *in Him* they are yes; wherefore also by Him is our Amen to the glory of God through us."

2 Corinthians 5:21
"He made Him who knew no sin to be sin on our behalf, that we might become the righteousness of God *in Him*."

2 Corinthians 13:4
"For indeed He was crucified because of weakness, yet

---

[5]The Nestle's Greek text has "through Jesus."

He lives because of the power of God. For we also are weak *in Him*, yet we shall live with Him because of the power of God directed toward you."

Ephesians 1:4
". . . He chose us *in Him* before the foundation of the world, that we should be holy and blameless. . . ."

Ephesians 1:9
"He made known to us the mystery of His will, according to His kind intention which He purposed *in Him*."

Ephesians 4:20, 21
"But you did not learn Christ in this way, if indeed you have heard Him and have been taught *in Him*, just as truth is in Jesus."

Philippians 3:8, 9
"More than that, I count all things to be loss in view of the surpassing value of knowing Christ Jesus my Lord, for whom I have suffered the loss of all things, and count them but rubbish in order that I may gain Christ, and may be found *in Him*, . . ."

Colossians 1:17
"And He is before all things, and *in Him* all things hold together."

Colossians 1:19
"For it was the Father's good pleasure for all the fulness to dwell *in Him*."

Colossians 2:6, 7
"As you therefore have received Christ Jesus the Lord, so walk *in Him*, having been firmly rooted and now

being built up *in Him* and established in your faith, just as you were instructed, and overflowing with gratitude."

Colossians 2:9
"For *in Him* all the fulness of Deity dwells in bodily form."

Colossians 2:10
"And *in Him* you have been made complete, and He is the head over all rule and authority."

2 Thessalonians 1:11, 12
"To this end also we pray for you always that our God may count you worthy of your calling, and fulfill every desire for goodness and the work of faith with power; in order that the name of our Lord Jesus may be glorified in you, and you *in Him*, according to the grace of our God and the Lord Jesus Christ."

1 John 2:27
"And as for you, the anointing which you received from Him abides in you, and you have no need for anyone to teach you; but as His anointing teaches you about all things, and is true and is not a lie, and just as it has taught you, you abide *in Him*."

1 John 2:28
"And now, little children, abide *in Him*, so that when He appears, we may have confidence and not shrink away from Him in shame at His coming."

1 John 3:24
"And the one who keeps His commandments abides *in Him*, and He in him. And we know by this that He

abides in us, by the Spirit whom He has given us."

1 John 4:13
"By this we know that we abide *in Him* and He in us, because He has given us of His Spirit."

1 John 5:20
"And we know that the Son of God has come, and has given us understanding, in order that we might know Him who is true, and we are *in Him* who is true, in His Son Jesus Christ. This is the true God and eternal life."

"Into Him" (1)

Ephesians 4:15
"But speaking the truth in love, we are to grow up in all aspects *into Him*, who is the head, even Christ."

"In whom" (10)

Ephesians 1:7
"In Him[6] we have redemption through His blood, the forgiveness of our trespasses, according to the riches of His grace."

Ephesians 1:11
"Also[7] we have obtained an inheritance, having been predestined according to His purpose who works all things after the counsel of His will."

Ephesians 1:13
"In Him,[8] you also, after listening to the message of

---

[6]Although the NASB has "in Him," the Nestle's Greek text has "in whom."

[7]The Nestle's Greek text has "in whom also. . . ."

[8]Although the NASB has "in Him" twice in this verse, the Nestle's Greek text has "in whom" in both cases.

truth, the gospel of your salvation—having also believed, you were sealed in Him with the Holy Spirit of promise."

Ephesians 2:21
"In whom the whole building, being fitted together is growing into a holy temple in the Lord."

Ephesians 2:22
"In whom you also are being built together into a dwelling of God in the Spirit."

Ephesians 3:12
"In whom we have boldness and confident access through faith in Him."

Colossians 1:14
"In whom we have redemption, the forgiveness of sins."

Colossians 2:3
"In whom are hidden all the treasures of wisdom and knowledge."

Colossians 2:11
"And in Him[9] you were also circumcised with a circumcision made without hands, in the removal of the body of the flesh by the circumcision of Christ."

"In His Son" (1)
1 John 5:11
"And the witness is this, that God has given us eternal life, and this life is *in His Son*."

---

[9]Although the NASB has "in Him," the Nestle's Greek text has "in whom."

"In His Son Jesus Christ" (1)

1 John 5:20

"And we know that the Son of God has come, and has given us understanding, in order that we might know Him who is true, and we are in Him who is true, *in His Son Jesus Christ.* This is the true God and eternal life."

"The body of Christ" (3)

Romans 7:4

"Therefore, my brethren, you also were made to die to the Law through *the body of Christ,* that you might be joined to another, to Him who was raised from the dead, that we might bear fruit for God."

1 Corinthians 10:16

"Is not the cup of blessing which we bless a sharing in the blood of Christ? Is not the bread which we break a sharing in *the body of Christ?*"

Ephesians 4:11, 12

"And He gave some as apostles, . . . for the equipping of the saints for the work of service, to the building up of *the body of Christ.*"

"Christ's body" (1)

1 Corinthians 12:27

"Now you are *Christ's body,* and individually members of it."

"His body" (3)

Ephesians 1:22, 23

"And He put all things in subjection under His feet, and gave Him as head over all things to the church, which is *His body,* the fulness of Him who fills all in all."

Ephesians 5:29, 30
"For no one ever hated his own flesh, but nourishes and cherishes it, just as Christ also does the church, because we are members of *His body.*"

Colossians 1:24
"Now I rejoice in my sufferings for your sake, and in my flesh I do my share on behalf of *His body* (which is the church) in filling up that which is lacking in Christ's afflictions."

"The body" (4)

Ephesians 3:6
". . . the Gentiles are fellow heirs and fellow members of *the body*,[10] and fellow partakers of the promise in Christ Jesus through the gospel."

Ephesians 5:23
"For the husband is the head of the wife, as Christ also is the head of the church, He Himself being the Savior of *the body.*"

Colossians 1:18
"He is also head of *the body*, the church; and He is the beginning, the first-born from the dead; so that He Himself might come to have first place in everything."

Colossians 2:18, 19
"Let no one keep defrauding you of your prize by delighting in self-abasement and the worship of the angels, . . . and not holding fast to the head, from whom *the* entire *body*, being supplied and held together by the

---

[10]The Nestle's Greek text has "joint-body."

joints and ligaments, grows with a growth which is from God."

"One body" (5)

Romans 12:5
"So we, who are many, are *one body* in Christ, and individually members one of another."

1 Corinthians 12:13
"For by one Spirit we were all baptized into *one body*, whether Jews or Greeks, whether slaves or free, and we were all made to drink of one Spirit."

Ephesians 2:14-16
"For He Himself is our peace, who made both groups into one, . . . and might reconcile them both in *one body* to God through the cross, by it having put to death the enmity."

Ephesians 4:4
"There is *one body* and one Spirit, just as also you were called in one hope of your calling."

Colossians 3:15
"And let the peace of Christ rule in your hearts, to which indeed you were called in *one body*; and be thankful."

Bibliography

Bales, J. D. *The Cross and the Church.* Shreveport, La.: Lambert Book House, 1974.

Bell, R. C. *Studies in Ephesians.* Austin, Tex.: Firm Foundation Publishing Company, 1971.

Bright, John. *The Kingdom of God.* Nashville, Tenn.: Abingdon, 1953.

Campbell, Alexander. *The Christian System.* St. Louis, Mo.: Christian Board of Publication, 1839; reprint, Cincinnati, Ohio: Standard Publishing Company, n.d.

Cogdill, Roy E. *The New Testament Church.* Lufkin, Tex.: R. E. Cogdill Publishing Company, 1946.

Elkins, Garland and Thomas B. Warren, eds. *The Church: The Beautiful Bride of Christ.* Jonesboro, Ark.: National Christian Press, 1980.

Ferguson, Everett. *The New Testament Church.* The Way of Life Series. Abilene, Tex.: Biblical Research Press, 1968.

Flew, R. N. *Jesus and His Church.* London: Epworth, 1943.

Genner, E. E. *The Church in the New Testament.* London: Charles H. Kelly, 1914.

Graves, W. C. *Lessons on the Church of Christ.* Birmingham, Al.: W. C. Graves, n.d.

Ladd, George Eldon. *Crucial Questions About the Kingdom of God.* Grand Rapids, Mich.: Wm. B. Eerdmans Publishing Company, 1952.

Milligan, Robert. *The Scheme of Redemption.* n.p., 1868; reprint, St. Louis, Mo.: The Bethany Press, 1962.

Minear, Paul. *Images of the Church in the New Testament.* Philadelphia: Westminster Press, 1960.

Paxson, Ruth. *The Wealth, Walk, and Warfare of the Christian.* Old Tappan, N.J.: Fleming H. Revell Company, 1939.

Phillips, Thomas W. *The Church of Christ.* Cincinnati, Ohio: Standard Publishing Company, 1943.

Schweizer, Eduard. *The Church as the Body of Christ.* Richmond, Va.: John Knox, 1964.

Stewart, James S. *A Man in Christ.* London: Hodder and Stoughton, 1947.

Stott, John R. W. *What Christ Thinks of the Church.* Grand Rapids, Mich.: Wm. B. Eerdmans Publishing Company, 1958.

Thomas, J. D., ed. *God's Eternal Purpose.* Abilene Christian College Book Store, 1969.

Wilson, L. R. *The New Testament Church: A Divine Institution.* Austin, Tex.: Firm Foundation Publishing Company, 1953.

ORDER INFORMATION

✉ **Postal Orders:** Resource Publications,
202 S. Locust, Searcy, AR 72143

For Further Information:
☎ **Telephone:** (501) 268-7588
✳ **Fax:** (501) 268-1472

Book 1: **What Is "the Church"?**

Book 2: **God's Design for "the Church"**
by
Eddie Cloer
1-9 books — $6.95 each
10 or more books —
Ask for discount information

Sales Tax: Please add 4.5% for books shipped to
Arkansas addresses.
Postage: 1-2 books—15% of total (4th Class)
3 or more books—8% of total (4th Class)
Handling: 1-2 books—$1.50
3 or more books—$1.00
Payment: Please make your check or money order
payable to Resource Publications.

Indicate if you wish to receive information on
other books which are available or information on
this year's Book Program.

Order now!